ADHESIVES
and
COATINGS

For over a decade, the Science for Conservators volumes have been the key basic texts for conservators throughout the world. Scientific concepts are fundamental to the conservation of artefacts of every type, yet many conservators have little or no scientific training. These introductory volumes provide non-scientists with the essential theoretical background to their work.

The Heritage: Care–Preservation–Management programme has been designed to serve the needs of the museum and heritage community worldwide. It publishes books and information services for professional museum and heritage workers, and for all the organizations that service the museum community.

Editor-in-chief: Andrew Wheatcroft

SCIENCE FOR CONSERVATORS
Volume 3
ADHESIVES
and
COATINGS

Conservation Science Teaching Series

MUSEUMS &
GALLERIES
COMMISSION

in conjunction with Routledge
London and New York

Scientific Editor

Jonathan Ashley-Smith
Keeper of Conservation
Victoria & Albert Museum

Series Editor (Books 1–3)

Helen Wilks

Adviser

Graham Weaver
Senior Lecturer
Department of Materials
Science
Faculty of Technology
Open University

Authors

Charles Newey
Ex-Professor of Materials Science
Faculty of Technology
Open University

Ruth Boff
Ex-Principal Scientific Officer
British Museum

Vincent Daniels
Principal Scientific Officer
British Museum

Michael Pascoe
Ex-Principal Lecturer and Head of Science
Camberwell School of Art and Crafts

Norman Tennant
Honorary Research Fellow
Department of Chemistry
University of Glasgow

Advisers

Suzanne Keene
Head of Collections Services Group
Science Museum

Helen Ganiaris
Conservation Officer
Museum of London

Kate Starling
Senior Conservation Officer
Museum of London

Jane McAusland
Private Conservator

First published by the Crafts Council 1983
Second impression 1984

Published by The Conservation Unit of the
Museums & Galleries Commission in 1987

New hardback and paperback edition published in 1992
by Routledge
11 New Fetter Lane, London EC4P 4EE

Simultaneously published in the USA and Canada
by Routledge
29 West 35th Street, New York, NY 10001

Reprinted 1994, 1996 and 1999

© 1987, 1992 Museums & Galleries Commission

Illustrations by Berry/Fallon Design
Designed by Robert Updegraff and Gillian Crossley-Holland

Printed in England by Butler & Tanner Ltd,
Frome and London

British Library Cataloguing in Publication Data
A catalogue record for this book is available
from the British Library

Library of Congress Cataloguing in Publication Data
A catalogue record for this book is available
from the Library of Congress

ISBN 0–415–07163–1

Contents

Preface to the 1992 edition

The science of conserving artworks and other items of cultural significance has undergone considerable change since 1982 when this series was instigated, mostly involving the development or application of new materials or techniques. Their understanding by conservators, restorers and students continues, nonetheless, to depend on familiarity with the underlying scientific principles which do not change and which are clearly explained in these books.

In response to continued international demand for this series, The Conservation Unit is pleased to be associated with Routledge in presenting these new editions as part of The Heritage: Care–Preservation–Management programme. The volumes are now enhanced by lists of recommended reading which will lead the reader to further helpful texts, developing scientific ideas in a conservation setting and bringing their application up to date.

Introduction

"Who are *you*?" said the Caterpillar.

This was not an encouraging opening for a conversation. Alice replied, rather shyly, "I – I hardly know, sir, just at present – at least I know who I *was* when I got up this morning, but I think I must have been changed several times since then."

"What do you mean by that?" said the Caterpillar sternly. "Explain yourself!"

"I can't explain *myself*, I'm afraid, sir," said Alice, "because I'm not myself, you see."

"I don't see," said the Caterpillar.

"I'm afraid I can't put it more clearly," Alice replied very politely, "for I can't understand it myself to begin with; and being so many different sizes in a day is very confusing."

"It isn't," said the Caterpillar.

"Well, perhaps you haven't found it so yet," said Alice; "but when you have to turn into a chrysalis – you will some day, you know – and then after that into a butterfly, I should think you'll feel it a little queer, won't you?"

"Not a bit," said the Caterpillar.

"Well, perhaps your feelings may be different," said Alice; "all I know is, it would feel very queer to *me*."

"You!" said the Caterpillar contemptuously. "Who are *you*?"

Alice's Adventures in Wonderland
Lewis Carroll, 1865

Faced with the enormous variety of molecular structures which create the different properties in materials, you might be forgiven for feeling as confused as Alice. Polymer chemistry is central to understanding the materials so often used in adhesives and coating and, in contrast to the unsympathetic attitude of the

Caterpillar, all it needs is a little simple explanation.

The main aim of this book, the third in the series, is to help you appreciate the underlying physics and chemistry of the processes involved in the joining, coating and consolidation of objects and of the various types of material you might use. It is *not* intended to be a practical handbook but aims to provide you with the scientific basis you need in order to read other specialist literature more effectively. It will not tell you, for instance, which adhesive to use for a particular repair, but by increasing your awareness and critical faculties it should help you to make a wise decision.

In contrast to cleaning (the subject of Book 2 in this series) which includes the *removal* of the material products of age and environment from an object, joining, coating and consolidation depend on the *addition* of new material. These three processes have other features in common, which makes it very useful to consider them together. First, the materials used as adhesives, coatings or consolidants usually need to meet similar technical requirements. For instance, to work effectively, a coating or consolidant should behave like an adhesive in that it should stick to the surface of the object with which it is in contact; much of the scientific understanding of how materials stick together is common to all three processes. Second, many of the materials used are polymers (very large molecules) of one sort or another. By studying the structure and properties of polymers in general, you can learn a lot about the effectiveness of particular polymeric materials in each of the three processes.

In defining the scope of this book, the properties of the materials *added* to an object have been emphasized but this is only part of the technical side of the problem. The addition of any material to an object will affect the object in some way, and this can raise a whole range of ethical problems. Can an adhesive or consolidant be removed without damaging the original object? It may, for example, be perfectly easy to dissolve a sample of a coating material in a beaker but impossible in practice to remove it from a textile or from porous stonework. Does the application of a material alter the information provided by an object? For instance, the temperatures required for joining metals by brazing can alter the microstructure of the object, so an organic adhesive might be preferable. Does the added material produce an unacceptable change in the appearance of the object? A coating may protect metal from corrosion, wood from loss of moisture, fabric or a painting from environmental degradation, but these advantages have to be weighed up against any resulting difference in appearance and tactile behaviour, as well as the risk of trapping harmful chemicals in the artefact – salts in stonework, for example.

Decisions about these and many other related questions have to be weighed against the need to join, coat or consolidate an object in order to prolong its life, to make it easier to handle, to prevent total deterioration, and so on. There are bound to be compromises – the strongest adhesive may be the most difficult to reverse; the surface coating least permeable to pollutant gases may give too much gloss to a silver object. But, again, appreciating the underlying science of the processes involved should help you in your decision-making.

Using This Book

This book is divided into three parts, joining, coating, and consolidation, and they are considered in that order. A number of scientific topics are relevant to all three processes, but to maintain a consistent and coherent development of the common science topics (such as the chemistry of polymers and the mechanical behaviour of solids) they are all introduced in the context of joining and dealt with there as fully as is needed for consideration of both joining and coating.

Structuring the book in this way means that the first part is by far the longest, but this does not mean that joining has been given a more comprehensive or deeper treatment. However, it does mean that if you are not familiar with the science covered in the first chapters, you are unlikely to understand Chapters 6 and 7. As with the other books in the series, the best way to use the book is to start at the beginning and work slowly through it.

Book 3 has also been written on the assumption that you are familiar with the scientific ideas and vocabulary already covered in Book 1, *An Introduction to Materials*, and Book 2, *Cleaning*. In particular, you will need to be familiar with the following subjects:

solubility, solutes and solvents (Book 2, Section 3B)

polar and non-polar molecules (Book 2, Sections 1C and 4A)

secondary bonds between molecules; dipole-dipole; Van der Waals; hydrogen bonds (Book 1, Sections 4C1 and 4D; Book 2, Sections 1C and 4B)

the types and formulae of common organic compounds, particularly alkanes, alkenes, alcohols, esters and ketones (Book 1, Section 5C; Book 2, Section 4B)

surface tension of liquids; how detergents work; the wetting of surfaces; hydrophilic and hydrophobic molecules (Book 2, Sections 3A2 and 5D)

oxidation and reduction (Book 2, Section 7B)

Simple demonstrations have been included to illustrate or clarify certain points in the text. New scientific words and terms are printed in bold type and are repeated in the outer margins for easy reference. Cross-references are given where it may help you to refer back to a previous passage (or to the earlier books in the series) and a full index is included at the end of the book.

1

Sticking things together

Sticking things together

In this chapter the question "What makes things stick together?" is tackled. The requirements of a good adhesive and a good joint are also considered, and, finally, the characteristics, advantages and disadvantages of the various types of adhesives used in conservation.

A How do things stick together?

The objects you deal with are integral entities, that is, they stay in one piece, because they are held together by the strong **cohesive forces** that stem from either ionic, covalent or metallic primary bonds between their constituent atoms (Book 1, Chapter 4), or from secondary bonds between their molecules (Book 2, Chapter 1). As you know from common experience of a broken object, a cup say, even if you fit the pieces back together very carefully they will not stick, and you can still see the line of the break. Although the thickness of this line can be extremely small — a fraction of a millimetre — it is still very large compared with the distance over which the cohesive forces act.

    One reason why the broken surfaces cannot be put back into intimate contact is that on a microscopic scale they are, in fact, very irregular. Even the fracture surface of a piece of glass, which we see with the naked eye as being extremely smooth, is revealed by a powerful microscope to be a mazy scene of ridges and valleys (see Figure 1.1). It is not surprising therefore that two such surfaces cannot be perfectly matched again: they will only make contact on a microscopic scale at rare points, and over most of the surface there will be air between the pieces.

cohesive forces

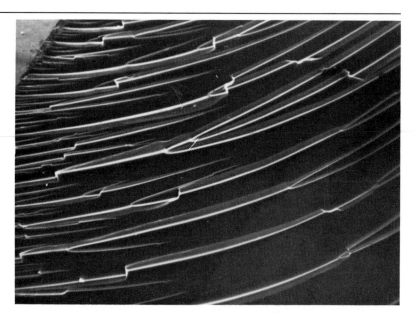

Figure 1.1 *The fracture surface of a piece of glass as seen through a powerful microscope, showing ridges and valleys.*

contaminated surfaces

Further, immediately an object is broken, the newly created fracture surfaces become **contaminated** by oxygen, water or other chemicals in the environment. Those atoms or molecules at the surface of the object that, prior to fracture, contributed to the cohesive forces in the material are now free to make bonds with the contaminant atoms or molecules. In this way metals oxidise by primary bonds being formed between metal and oxygen atoms; water molecules from the atmosphere hydrogen-bond to materials such as paper and wood leading to a thin layer of moisture on the surface, and so on. Processes like these are the ones that have to be reversed when an object is cleaned. Surface contaminants *adhere,* via primary or secondary bonds, to a fracture surface, and so they inhibit the re-joining of the broken pieces.

Since the broken surfaces will not join themselves together, another way must be found. Basically, there are two ways by which bits of solid materials can be joined together:

1 Using some sort of device that mechanically locks the pieces together. (Mechanical in this context means non-chemical.)

adhesive 2 Using an **adhesive**; that is, a material which, ideally, fills the gaps between the pieces, adheres to both surfaces and achieves a sufficiently strong and rigid interface between the pieces.

Sewing torn pieces of fabric together is an obvious example of mechanical locking, and so is the use of screws, rivets and dowels.

The joining mechanism does not depend on any primary or secondary bonding between the locking device and the pieces of the object. Of course, chemical reactions may occur with time; the rusting of screws, and the rotting of threads are examples which may lead to breakdown of the joint.

Adhesives have been the subject of considerable scientific research, but exactly how they bond to solids is still not clearly understood. It is thought that adhesion is due to secondary bonding between the molecules in the adhesive and the atoms or molecules at the surface of the pieces to be joined (the **adherend** or *substrate*). Clearly, the magnitude of these forces is an important factor in determining the strength of the resulting joint. Nowadays, following the development of a wide variety of synthetic polymers, a multitude of new adhesives of this type is available in addition to the traditional natural polymeric adhesives made from animal hide and bone, starch, cellulose, and so on.

Some adhesives are formed by chemical reactions *in situ* between different ingredients. This happens, for instance, with epoxy resins and cyanoacrylate adhesives. Of course, in a chemical reaction, primary bonds in the starting materials are broken and new ones are made to form the products of the reaction. Even with these adhesives it is thought that no new primary bonds are formed *across* the interface between the adhesive and the solid surface, but that adhesion is essentially by means of secondary bonds.

In some particular cases the joining process does produce primary bonding right across the interface, so much so that the original interface disappears. This happens, for instance, when a joint is made by locally melting the two pieces and holding them together until they resolidify; examples are brazing and welding. Figure 1.2 is an illustration of how the interface is destroyed by welding. From

adherend

Figure 1.2 *A photomicrograph of a welded joint, showing how an interface between two pieces of metal has been destroyed by fusion.*

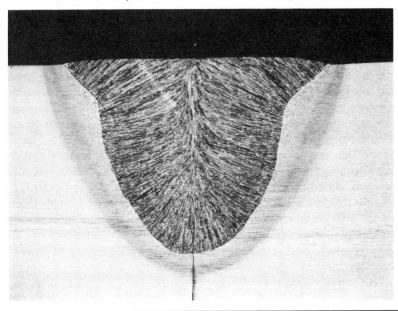

a conservation viewpoint, such a technique has some obvious undesirable features.

The difference between the two ways of joining – by mechanical locking or by an adhesive – becomes rather blurred when you consider how an adhesive works at a microscopic level. In fact, in many **mechanical interlocking** cases, **mechanical interlocking** may contribute significantly to the effectiveness of an adhesive. If you look again at the glass fracture surface illustrated in Figure 1.1, you will appreciate that a suitable adhesive could penetrate the nooks and crannies on the surface, and also the surface to which it is to be joined, and thus produce an interlocking of the fragments. Similarly, pieces of paper or fabric can be joined by an adhesive that penetrates between the fibres. The pieces are held together by the veins of adhesive, which act as hooks around the paper or textile fibres, as in Velcro.

In the context of this book there is no need to pursue the details of theories of adhesion any further, however the basic mechanisms of secondary bonding and microscopic interlocking just described will enlighten later discussions. In the next section the characteristics that an adhesive and the surfaces to be joined should have in order to produce a satisfactory joint are explored.

B What is needed to make a good joint?

What is meant by a good joint really depends on the meaning of "good". It involves a balance between judgements about the quality of the joint on technical, aesthetic and ethical grounds, the required properties of the adhesive, and the efficiency with which the joint is made.

At this point it is important to appreciate that in discussing different types of adhesive, and the science relating to them, there is a very particular definition of "good" when considering adhesives for conservation work. Most modern adhesives have been developed to produce joints that are good in terms of the criteria of mass-production manufacturing industries – furniture production, car production and so on. This has meant that the search has been for adhesives that produce very strong joints – indeed with many modern adhesives the material of which the object is made may break, rather than the joint. Further, the requirement is for joints which resist degradation in use caused by chemicals in the environment. This usually means that joints produced by such adhesives are difficult to reverse by, for example, dissolving in common solvents such as water and simple organic liquids. These needs for strong, chemically indestructible adhesives are usually at odds with those of the conservator, who often wishes to make a glued joint which holds the pieces of an object together satisfactorily but which can be readily taken apart at some future time without damaging its characteristics.

Although these very different requirements are quite obvious, ways of considering the scientific background to adhesives in the context of conservation are *not*. For instance, it is more straight-forward to analyse the factors that produce a *strong* joint rather than those that produce a *weak* joint. This is the approach taken here, with, where appropriate, a discussion of the special requirements of adhesives in conservation work.

Think of an object that needs to be mended. What are the important requirements of the joint you intend to make? What are the steps in making the joint that need the most careful attention?

The diagram in Figure 1.3 attempts to cover the main points you should have considered. Notice that many of the factors have implications for others. For example, making a joint strong may not be compatible with the necessity to remove (take down) the joint without harming the object, and an invisible join may soon become visible due to discoloration. All of the topics in Figure 1.3 (except the need to have clean surfaces) have implications for the type of adhesive you use; they can be used to draw up a specification of the desirable properties of an adhesive. However, there may be additional constraints put on the choice of adhesive, such as cost and whether it presents hazards to the conservator, for example by releasing noxious fumes.

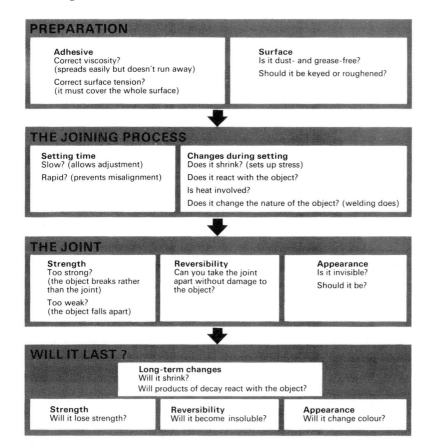

Figure 1.3 *Factors to be considered when joining an object during conservation treatment.*

You will now be aware that the selection of the best adhesive is a complex problem. Of course, for a particular job some of these factors may be irrelevant or easy to decide, but, even so, a large number of variable and inter-related factors will remain. Having considered the problem in a general way, you can now start to analyse the main factors in more detail, using the items in Figure 1.3 as a guide. A convenient starting point is with the need for the adhesive to be spread over the whole of the surfaces to be joined.

C Helping the adhesive to do its job

Whatever the mechanism of adhesion it is self-evident that the greater the area of intimate contact between an adhesive and the object, the more effectively will the surfaces be stuck together. This is simply because the greater the area of contact, the more bonding sites there are. To obtain a maximum contact area, three things are important:

1 The surfaces must be as clean as possible, that is as free as possible from chemicals that obstruct bonding between the adhesive and the adherend. Any dirt or loose pieces of the object not firmly attached to the surfaces will mask the underlying surfaces and prevent contact by the adhesive.

2 The rougher the surfaces are the better, because the surface area is greater than for a smooth surface, and because interlocking of the surface and the adhesive is increased. This is why the instructions on the containers for many proprietary adhesives tell you to roughen the surfaces to be joined. Such treatment is not appropriate for most conservation work, but it may be useful to know that roughening materials such as wood and leather raises some of their fibres proud of the surface, thus giving enhanced bonding by being embedded in the adhesive.

3 To achieve close contact and spread over the surfaces, the adhesive must *wet* the surfaces, and be liquid enough to flow into pores and crevices in the surfaces.

surface tension As you know, from Book 2, whether a liquid wets a solid or not depends on its **surface tension**. The lower the surface tension of a liquid the easier it is for a droplet to spread and wet the surface of a solid. If there are strong forces of attraction between molecules in the liquid and the solid, the liquid will wet the solid surface. If, however, the secondary bonding within the liquid is stronger than the bonding between liquid and solid, then droplets will be formed that do not spread to cover the surface.

You can demonstrate this by dropping water onto a clean (degreased) sheet of glass and onto a piece of glass that has been smeared with candle wax.

As the sticking power of adhesives depends on secondary bonding to the solid surface, the majority of adhesives have strongly **polar groups** in their molecules (see Book 2, Section 4B). If the surfaces to be joined are contaminated with non-polar substances such as grease, the adhesive will not spread.

polar groups

So far only flat surfaces have been considered. The extent to which a liquid penetrates an irregular surface depends on another phenomenon related to surface tension: **capillary action**. You take advantage of this effect whenever you use absorbent materials to soak up liquids – paper tissues, dishcloths, and towels for instance. These materials consist of a network of fibres, and liquids soak into them by being drawn along the narrow interstices between the fibres by capillary action. The same effect occurs in thin tubes when they are dipped in most liquids; the liquid rises up the tube. Such tubes are called capillaries. The pores, cracks, scratches or pits on the surface of an object can also act like capillaries.

capillary action

For capillary action to take place the liquid must wet the surface of the solid; the adhesion between the liquid and the solid is then greater than the cohesion of the liquid. This means that the liquid/ air interface (the **meniscus**) is curved downwards because the (secondary) forces of adhesion between the liquid and the material of the tube pull the liquid up the sides of the solid surfaces. This is illustrated for capillary tubes in Figure 1.4.

meniscus

The liquid rises until the upward pull is balanced by the gravitational pull on the liquid in the tube, Figure 1.4(a). Another important feature of capillary action is that the wider the capillary, the smaller is the capillary rise, as in Figure 1.4(b). This follows from the balance between the upward force and the weight of liquid in the tube.

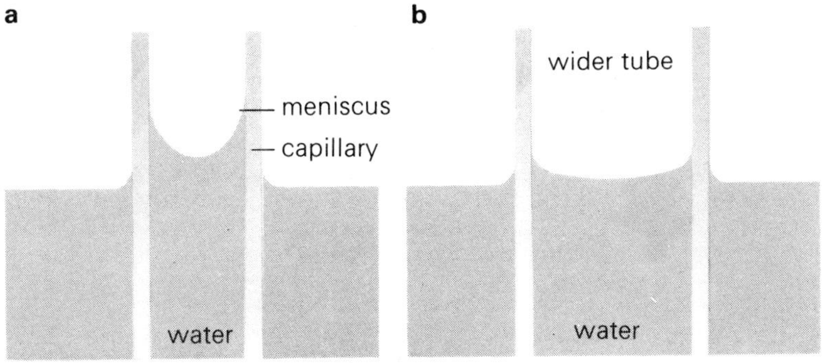

Figure 1.4 *Differing levels of liquid within two capillaries, caused by their varying widths.*

This is not the end of the story, however. In order to flow over a surface, a liquid has to be runny. The resistance a liquid offers to flowing is called its **viscosity**, and was discussed in Book 2 (Chapter 3). In general, the larger the molecules in a liquid the stronger the secondary bonding between them, and the greater is the viscosity. The lower the viscosity, the more readily will a liquid

viscosity

spread. From everyday experience, you know that the viscosities of solids are extremely high compared with liquids; solids do not flow.

You can probably see the importance of the need for an adhesive **wettability** to **wet** the surfaces of the adherend, and to have a low viscosity. The adhesive then makes intimate contact with the surfaces and penetrates the irregularities on them. Up to a certain size, the wider the pores, hollows, and so on, the less they will be penetrated. It clearly follows that, at this stage, the adhesive has to be in the form of a liquid. But intuitively you know that finally the adhesive must be solid.

Demonstration

Obtain four ordinary glass microscope slides and carefully clean one face of each by washing them in acetone and leaving them to dry. Being careful not to touch the cleaned faces (grease from your fingers will destroy the effect you are seeking), put a few drops of water on the cleaned surfaces of two of the slides. Place one of the other cleaned slides on top of each of the wetted ones and press the pairs together. You should now have two pairs of slides, each with a thin film of water between them.

Take one of the pairs and try to part them by pulling them at right-angles to each slide (see Figure 1.5(a)). You will find that it is very difficult. The resistance to your pull is due to the surface tension of the water which attempts to minimise the liquid/air interface. If you drop the slides into a bowl of water they will separate more easily since surface tension exists only at the surface.

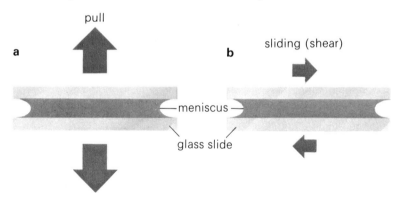

Figure 1.5

Now take the other pair of glass slides and try to part them by sliding them over one another (Figure 1.5(b)). This time you will find it very easy to part the slides. In this case, surface tension does not provide resistance to your shearing action because, as you will notice, the two menisci remain intact as the slides move past one another. The water continues to adhere to the glass, so the shearing movement must occur within the film of water. This is because the water molecules can move past one another very easily. (The ability to flow fairly readily is one of the characteristics that distinguishes a liquid from a solid.) You can demonstrate the difference between the two forms for water with one of your pairs of slides.

Put the slides in a deep freeze or the ice compartment of a refrigerator until the water becomes ice, and then try to part the slides by both pulling and sliding. You will find both tasks difficult, particularly the sliding one. When you pull the slides apart you will probably find that it does so by cracking along the interface between the ice and the glass; your pull has broken the adhesive bond.

The background to one of the fundamental problems of adhesives has now been outlined: to wet the surfaces, the adhesive must be a liquid, and to form a strong joint it needs to be a solid. In practice, the adhesive is applied in the form of a liquid and then modified to produce a solid. Basically, there are three ways of doing this.

1 **Melt-freeze adhesives.** The adhesive is prepared as a solid, is heated and applied to the surfaces to be joined as a molten liquid, then allowed to freeze back to a solid. Examples of this type of adhesive used in conservation are waxes such as beeswax, some animal glues, soldering and brazing. **melt-freeze adhesives**

2 **Solution adhesives.** Here, the intended adhesive material is dissolved in a suitable liquid solvent. After the solution has been applied to the surfaces, the solvent evaporates, leaving the solid adhesive behind. Examples of this type are starch-based glues, shellac (dissolved in alcohol), gum arabic (dissolved in water or saliva), rubber solution (for repairing bicycle inner-tubes), and cellulose nitrate. A variant of this type is to have the adhesive as a powder that is mixed with a suitable liquid to produce a **dispersion.** (Emulsions, slurries and pastes are forms of a dispersion.) Again, the liquid evaporates to leave the solid. An example in conservation work is polyvinyl acetate emulsion (PVAC). **solution adhesives**

dispersion

3 **Reaction adhesives.** In this type, two or more liquid compounds are mixed and applied to the surfaces to be joined; the chemicals react to produce a solid adhesive. Common modern examples of this type are based on epoxy resins (for example, Araldite) and urea formaldehyde (for example, Cascamite) resins. Many of them release water or other low molecular mass compounds during the final hardening process. **reaction adhesives**

Most adhesives used these days are synthetic polymers of one sort or another, and there are many sorts. Many of the traditional adhesives, some of which are still used and others you may come across in objects that have been repaired previously, are based on naturally occurring polymers such as starch, cellulose, rubber (latex), and proteins obtained from bones or plants. In order to continue this analysis of factors involved in making a good joint, you need to be familiar with some of the scientific models used to interpret the structure and behaviour of polymeric materials. This is the subject of the next chapter.

2

The chemistry of polymers

The chemistry of polymers

Polymer is the name given to very large molecules which contain hundreds, thousands, or even millions of atoms and are made up by the successive linking together of one or more types of small molecule. The small molecules are called **monomers** (from Greek words meaning single part) and they produce a polymer (many parts). Most of the properties of a polymer are strongly influenced by the way in which it is built up from its component monomers, and to help draw out this point it is useful to classify polymers into two types: those which form **long-chain molecules** and those which form one large continuous molecule consisting of a two- or three-dimensional network, that is, **network polymers**. In this chapter we will look at each of these in turn.

polymer

monomer

long-chain molecules

network polymers

A Long-chain polymers

These have the simplest structure and can be envisaged as a poppet-bead necklace in which the monomers are the poppet-beads each of which has a stud that links to another bead, so enabling the long-chain polymer to be built up.

Figure 2.1 *Schematic representation of monomers (poppet beads) joining to form a polymer (necklace).*

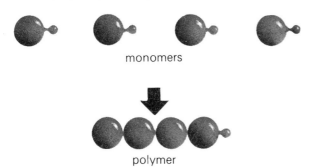

monomers

polymer

covalent bond   The simplest polymer like this is polyethylene. As its name implies, the monomer is ethylene. It has a double **covalent bond**:

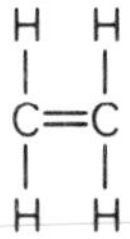

$$
\begin{array}{cc}
H & H \\
| & | \\
C & = C \\
| & | \\
H & H
\end{array}
$$

between the carbon atoms (see Book 1, Section 4C) which is highly reactive. In effect, one of these bonds provides the poppet-stud which links to a neighbouring molecule, which links to the next and so on, to create the long-chain polymer (Figure 2.2).

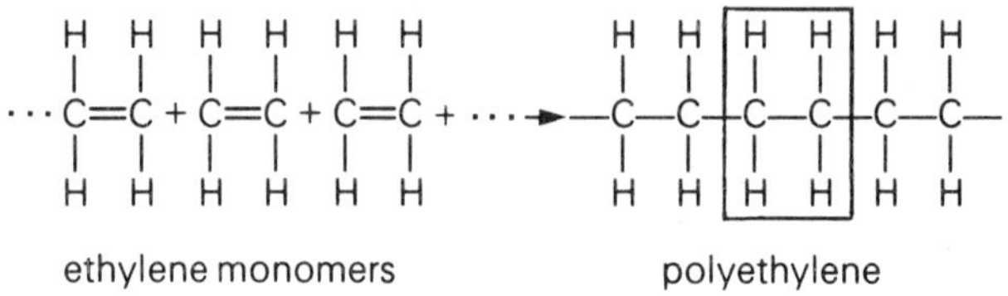

ethylene monomers   polyethylene

Figure 2.2

polymerisation   The chemical process of joining the monomers together is called **polymerisation**. This will be looked at a bit more closely in the next section. Polyethylene is a synthetic polymer which was first produced commercially in the late 1930s. It is the basis of one of the most widely used plastics, polythene, which you meet as plastic bags and all sorts of packaging and containers. In common usage *polyethylene* is now called *polythene*. Although the words *polymer* and *plastic* tend to be used synonymously, strictly they have different meanings. A polymer is a large molecule; a plastic is a product consisting of a mixture of polymer(s) with a variety of materials added for specific purposes, such as pigments, compounds to inhibit breakdown of the polymer by light or oxidation, **plasticisers** to

plasticisers   facilitate shaping and to make the product softer, and so on. Some of these additional constituents can cause ageing problems in adhesives and coatings, and examples of this are dealt with in Chapter 5.

A structural formula is a useful way of showing, schematically, how the atoms are disposed in a covalently bonded molecule. In Book 1 (Chapter 4) you were warned of the limitations of this type of model. It does not give much idea of what a polymer molecule actually looks like. For instance, a carbon atom is larger than a hydrogen atom. Further, the structural formula model implies that a long-chain polymer is straight and stiff; a real molecule is usually flexible and contorted. Although the C–C covalent bond is strong and fixed in direction, the kinetic energy possessed by the molecule allows rotation of the atoms about these bonds – just as poppet-beads can rotate about the studs.

The poppet-bead necklace (although, perhaps, a dated fashion) is quite a good analogy for a long-chain molecule with the beads as the carbon atoms. Adding two small balls to each bead to represent the hydrogen atoms would provide a better representation, although still approximate, of the molecule (see Figure 2.3).

Figure 2.3 *Model of a polyethylene molecule. The carbon atoms are black and the hydrogen atoms are white.*

Other long-chain polymers can be described using polyethylene as a basis. As an example, Figure 2.4 depicts the formation of polyvinyl chloride (PVC). The monomer is vinyl chloride.

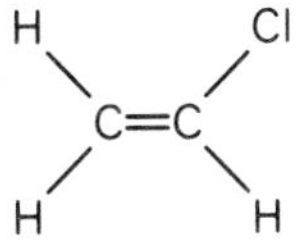

Vinyl chloride can be visualised as ethylene with a side-group of one hydrogen atom being replaced by a chlorine atom.

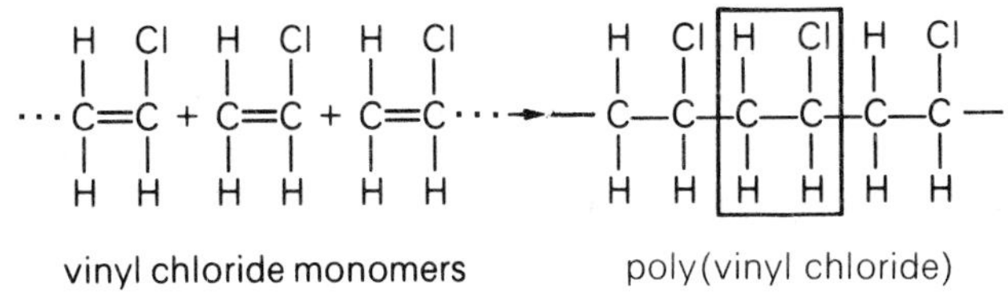

Figure 2.4

Many other long-chain polymers can be described in the same way. Figure 2.5 gives some examples that form the basis of important commercial plastics, including adhesives.

Structural formula	Monomer	Other names
polystyrene (PS)	styrene	Lustrex Styrofoam
poly(vinyl alcohol) (PVAL)	vinyl alcohol does not exist as a monomer. PVAL is made from PVAC	PVA, PVOH
poly(vinyl acetate) (PVAC)	vinyl acetate	often called PVA and confused with poly(vinyl alcohol)
Polyisoprene (natural rubber)	isoprene (2-methyl 1.3 butadiene)	latex
	tetrafluorethylene	Teflon Fluon
poly(methyl methacrylate) (PMMA)	methyl methacrylate	Perspex Plexiglas acrylic

You may be perplexed by the names of some of the polymers listed in Figure 2.5. Some of the difficulty arises from the variety and complexity of the materials themselves and is made worse by the lack of a universally agreed system for naming them. Thus, some are named after part, or all, of their chemical constituents (as are all of those in Figure 2.5), others have uninformative and inaccurate chemical names (for example, acrylic) others are proprietary names that have entered our vocabulary (for example, celluloid and nylon). A systematic method of naming is needed, and in recent years a step has been made in the right direction with the adoption of standard abbreviations. Those given in Figure 2.5 and others you will meet later in the text are used, for instance, by the British Standards Institution (BSI), the American Society for Testing and Materials (ASTM), and the International Union of Pure and Applied Chemistry (IUPAC). You should get into the habit of using these standard abbreviations; it will help, for example, to clear up the confusion about the ambiguous initials PVA, which can refer to a product based on **poly(vinyl acetate)** (PVAC) or **poly(vinyl alcohol)** (PVAL).

poly(vinyl acetate)
poly(vinyl alcohol)

There are many reasons for the commercial development of so many types of synthetic polymeric materials, but one of the most important is that different types of molecule produce different properties in the bulk material. One of the technological aims of their development is to produce polymers that carry out particular functions, or that do them better than alternative materials.

Imagine, for example, a mass of polymer made up of polyethylene (PE) molecules and another made of polymethylmethacrylate (PMMA) molecules. Both materials will contain large numbers of long-chain molecules, but the types of molecule are very different. PE molecules have only hydrogen side-groups attached to the carbon backbone, and, as you know, these are non-polar groups and only very weak secondary forces are set up between neighbouring molecules. As a direct consequence the molecules can be drawn apart quite readily, which means that PE has a low melting point, and is relatively soft and flexible (see Book 2 Section 4B). On the other hand, PMMA has some large polar side-groups which means that the molecules are irregular in shape and more strongly bound to one another. Thus, PMMA has higher melting point than PE and is harder and more rigid. This is the polymer from which Perspex (Plexiglas) is made.

So far only long-chain polymers that have a backbone composed solely of carbon atoms have been considered. However, the possibility of substituting other atoms for carbon in the backbone provides many other variations. The requirements are that the substitute atoms form at least two covalent bonds with neighbouring atoms so that the chain is maintained. Examples are oxygen, nitrogen, sulphur and silicon. The molecular structures can be quite complex: Figure 2.6 shows three relatively simple examples.

Figure 2.5 *Examples of the long chain polymers which are in common commercial use as plastics and adhesives.*

Type	Example	Structure
polyamide	Nylon 6	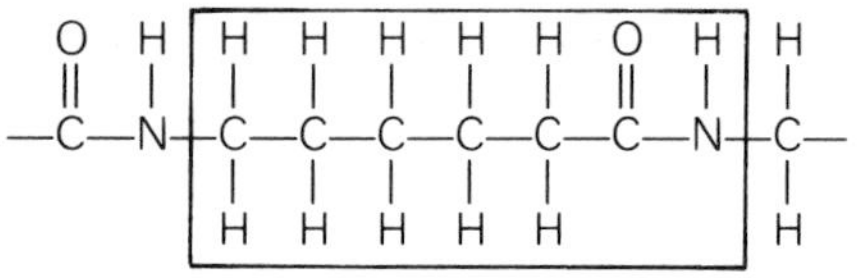
polyester	poly(ethylene terephthalate) for example, Terylene, Dacron	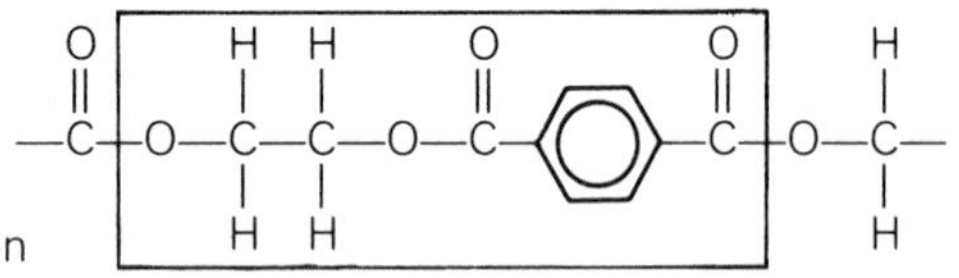
silicone (siloxane)		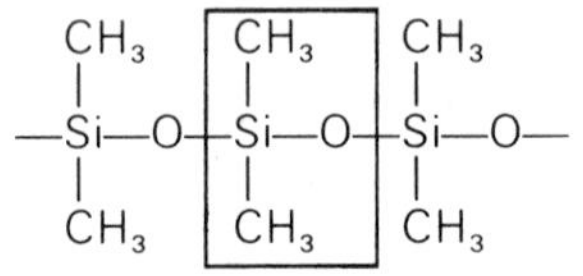

Figure 2.6 *Examples of polymers with carbon atoms substituted in the chain by other atoms: nitrogen, oxygen and silicon, respectively.*

The last of these examples is a member of the silicone family, that is, polymers in which silicon atoms take the place of some or all of the carbon atoms. Polyesters and silicones can exist as both long-chain or network polymers, and so they crop up again in the next section. There is a range of different nylons, which are distinguished by a number that indicates the number of successive carbon atoms in the backbone of the monomer(s). Some **nylons** are described by a single-digit number – for example, Nylon 6 which means the polymer was made from a single monomer containing six carbon atoms. Other nylons are described by a larger number – for example, Nylon 610 which means that the polymer is made from two different monomers, one containing six carbon atoms and another containing ten. Polymers made from more than one kind of monomer are called **co-polymers**.

nylon

co-polymers

A number of co-polymers play important roles in conservation work. For example Paraloid B72, which is used as a picture and metal varnish and also as a consolidation agent, is a co-polymer of methyl acrylate and ethyl methacrylate. Here, juggling the relative numbers of the methyl (CH_3—) side-group and the larger ethyl (C_2H_5—) side-group is used as a way of achieving desirable properties, such as the viscosity of the liquid varnish and toughness in the dried coating. Beva, the adhesive used in the lining and consolidation of paintings, is a co-polymer of ethylene and vinyl acetate together with a variety of other compounds each of which is added to achieve specific modifications of the properties of the plain co-polymer. The ubiquitous adhesive often known as PVA is a co-polymer of vinyl acetate with esters of maleic acid such as dibutyl maleate.

$$C_4H_9-\overset{\overset{\displaystyle O}{\|}}{C}-O \qquad O-\overset{\overset{\displaystyle O}{\|}}{C}-C_4H_9$$

$$\underset{H}{\overset{}{\diagup}}C=C\underset{H}{\overset{}{\diagdown}}$$

The repeated units in a co-polymer can be arranged in different ways, again leading to changes in properties. there are three main types: the **alternating co-polymer**, the **random** co-polymer, and the **block** co-polymer; they are illustrated schematically in Figure 2.7. Co-polymers with at least three basic units are made synthetically, and of course, in Nature, proteins are co-polymers of up to 21 amino acids.

alternating, random and block co-polymers

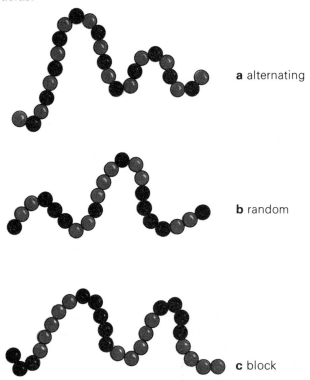

a alternating

b random

c block

Figure 2.7 *Schematic representation of alternating, random and block co-polymers.*

We have now discussed the basic types of long-chain polymers. Most are made synthetically; Nature prefers network polymers. However, some long-chain polymers do exist in Nature, for instance bitumen (a complex mixture of hydrocarbons) and cellulose (a major structural component of plants).

Before looking at network polymers it will help if you first consider the mechanisms of making long-chain polymers, that is, of *polymerisation*.

B Polymerisation

Molecules like ethylene and methyl methacrylate can be persuaded by chemical means to join together consecutively using one of the bonds in the double carbon bond, $C = C$. In principle any monomer with a double bond between carbon atoms can be polymerised in this way; it is called **addition polymerisation**. Notice that the polymer is the sole product of this sort of reaction (apart, of course, from a great deal of heat).

addition polymerisation

Some long-chain polymers, and network polymers, are produced by a chemical reaction called **condensation polymerisation**. The formation of the peptide link is a typical example of a condensation reaction (see Book 2, Chapter 7). In such a reaction two different sorts of molecule react to form the desired product as well as a small molecule as a by-product which is usually, but not always, water. The long-chain polymers called nylon and polyester, and also cellulose and proteins, are polymerised by successive condensation reactions. As an example let us analyse the formation of the polyester shown in Figure 2.5; it is available commercially as fibres (for example, Terylene) and films (Melinex and Mylar).

condensation polymerisation

It is made from two monomers, terephthalic acid which has the structural formula:

and has two acid side-groups:

and ethanediol (ethylene glycol – used in antifreeze) which has two hydroxyl (—OH) side-groups.

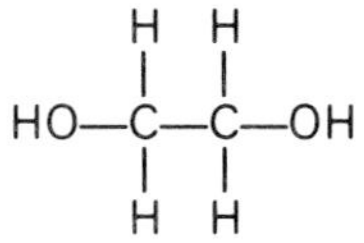

$$\begin{array}{c} \ \ \ \ \ H \ \ H \\ \ \ \ \ \ | \ \ \ | \\ HO-C-C-OH \\ \ \ \ \ \ | \ \ \ | \\ \ \ \ \ \ H \ \ H \end{array}$$

Acid and hydroxyl side-groups are strongly polar and they are the ones involved in the reaction between the two monomers. The first condensation reaction is then given by:

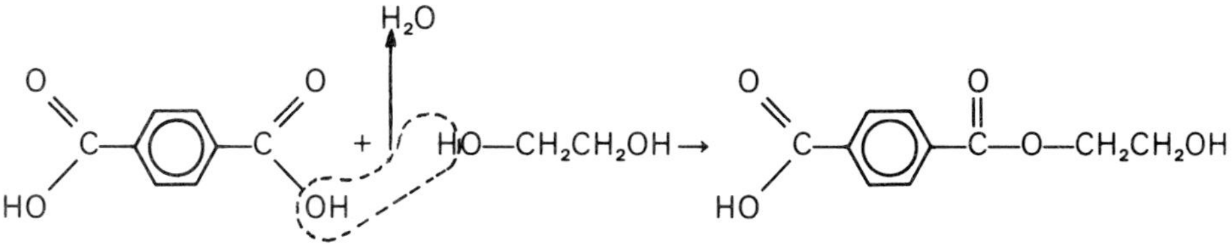

A hydrogen atom from the hydroxyl group combines with an —OH from an acid side-group to form a molecule of water (H_2O) which is released.

The molecule that is the product of the reaction still has reactive groups at each end which can react further with the monomers; the

ethanediol (glycol) reacts with the $-C\!\!\diagup^{\textstyle O}_{\diagdown OH}$ end, and the

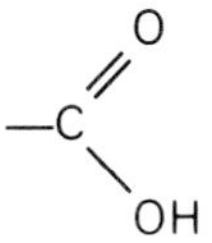

terephthalic acid reacts with the —OH end. Concentrating on the right-hand (— OH) side of the molecule, if the acid monomer reacts with it, followed by the diol monomer, the following is produced:

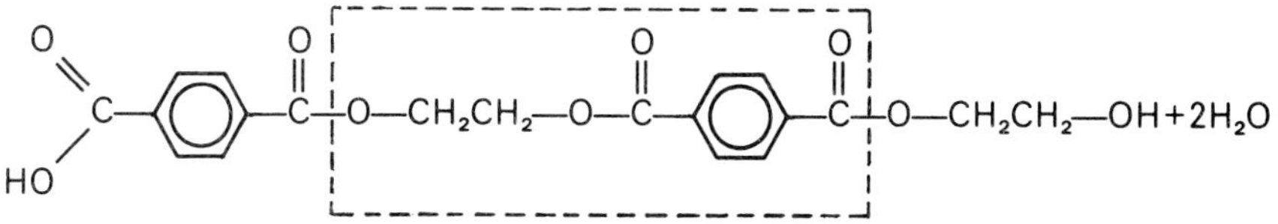

These condensation reactions continue, releasing a molecule of H_2O each time, to give a long-chain polymer.

Amongst others, nylons and cellulose are produced in the same way. Since cellulose-based adhesives are often used in conservation work, the formation of cellulose will be considered in some detail; its molecular structure and polymerisation are rather complicated and the description given here is much simplified.

The *cell*ular structure of plants is built up from *cell*ulose, and the amount of **cellulose** varies from one type of plant to another; the **cellulose** "linters" in cotton plants are virtually all cellulose whereas woods

lignin are only about 40 per cent cellulose (the other major component being **lignin**, a network polymer). Cellulose is a polymer of glucose, a sugar, which has the chemical formula $C_6H_{12}O_6$ and structural formula:

Again, the reactive —OH (hydroxyl) side-groups are involved in condensation reactions; you will notice that there are five of them in the glucose molecule. The glucose monomer can react to form a range of different polymers – starch, for instance, contains two polymers of glucose called amylopectin and amylose. The first is a linear polymer; the second, which is the major component, has a branched structure. It is the many reactive sites on the ends of the branches that make starch such an effective adhesive. In cellulose the repeat unit is two glucose molecules which are bonded together with one unit turned upside down with respect to the other, as follows. (For simplicity the carbon and single hydrogen atoms have been left out.):

This process is continued by further condensation reactions, each releasing a molecule of H_2O. A typical cellulose molecule contains as many as 10,000 glucose units. It is the —OH (hydroxyl) on the left- and right-hand sides of the glucose molecule in the diagram that take part in the polymerisation reactions. In the cellulose polymer, each glucose ring still has three —OH groups. The hydrogen-bonding between these groups, which are highly polar, provides strong bonding between neighbouring polymer molecules.

The hydroxyl groups can be attacked by nitric acid (HNO_3) converting them to a nitrate group (—NO_3). Being bulkier than —OH groups, the nitrate groups force the polymer chains further apart. If all the hydroxyl groups are replaced in this way, the result is gun-cotton – an explosive. Controlling the *nitration* so that, on average, two of the —OH groups on each glucose ring are replaced by —NO_3 yields cellulose nitrate (incorrectly known as nitrocellulose) which has been used as an adhesive for many years (dissolved in ketones or esters) and was the material used originally as the base for photographic film but is highly unstable.

nitration

It should be emphasised again that using the structural formula of a polymer is adequate for the *present* purpose of depicting the covalent bonds in the chain, but that real polymers *actually look* very different. They are three-dimensional, not two-dimensional; the chains are usually not straight; and depending on the size of the side-groups they can be "knobbly". Extensive studies of cellulose have shown that it is a long-chain molecule and Figure 2.8 is a close approximation to a very small part of it.

Figure 2.8 *Schematic representation of a cellulose molecule, showing its long chain form.*

C Network polymers

In contrast to a long-chain polymer, a **network polymer** can form bulk material that is composed of a continuous three-dimensional molecule, the whole of which is bound together by primary bonds.

network polymer

Therefore, network polymeric materials have very different properties from those consisting of many long-chain molecules. The structure cannot be disrupted so readily by heat, solvents or mechanical forces. There are many kinds of this type of material, both synthetic and natural, from Bakelite to proteins. Such networks can be created in two basic ways:

1 The linking of long-chains by atoms or small molecules.

2 Interaction between small molecules to produce branched chains that join together.

An important example of the first method is the vulcanising of rubber. Natural rubber, poly-isoprene, is a hydrocarbon consisting of long-chain molecules (see Figure 2.5). These chains can be linked together by sulphur atoms similar to the links between cysteine groups in proteins (see Book 2, Chapter 7):

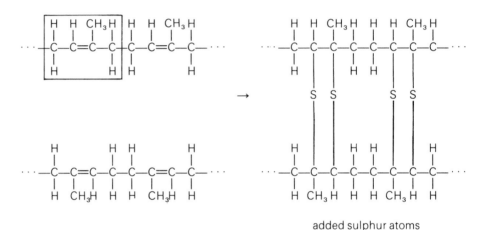

added sulphur atoms

Figure 2.9 *One way in which polyisoprene (natural rubber) chains can become covalently bonded together by cross-linking sulphur atoms to build a network.*

cross-linking

Each sulphur atom forms a **cross-link** between two chains by forming a covalent bond with each; in this case using the double-bond available in the isoprene unit. The availability of a double-bond in the chain is necessary for this method of building a network. Natural rubber is soft and sticky, but a typical rubber used in car tyres contains about 5 per cent sulphur, which produces a network with about 500 carbon atoms between cross-links. 40 per cent sulphur produces many more cross-links and results in a hard, rigid plastic, for instance Vulcanite and Ebonite. You can see from this that the degree of cross-linking has a dramatic effect on the properties of the polymer.

Earlier the polyester made of polyethylene terephthalate was considered as an example of long-chain molecules produced by condensation polymerisation. Similar long molecules can also be cross-linked to produce a network polyester. In order to do this the long-chain polyester molecules must be *unsaturated*, that is, contain double-bonds. This means that the monomer from which the long chain is formed must contain a carbon to carbon double-bond. One of the bonds in the double-bond in the long chain can be used to create a cross-link with an identical site on a neighbouring chain. Just as sulphur atoms provide the cross-links in vulcanised rubber, a monomer such as styrene:

can provide cross-links between the unsaturated long-chain polyester molecules. The result is a hard glossy material that is used as a casting resin, and in large quantities in "glass-reinforced plastics" (GRP). In practice, the long-chain polyester material is dissolved in styrene to form a viscous syrup. Just before use the *hardener* (a catalyst), which initiates and maintains the cross-linking process, is mixed into it. The epoxy resins form network polymers in a similar way. In all of these examples, vulcanised rubber, polyesters and epoxy resins, the cross-linking occurs by **addition polymerisation**, and so no by-product is generated. Similar cross-linking of long-chain molecules also occurs in many proteins, for example in **collagen** (a main component of bone, tendon, skin and hence leather) and in **keratin** (feather, hair and horn).

addition polymerisation

collagen
keratin

The second way of producing network polymers, that is, by the interaction of small molecules that generate branched chains that link up, involves successive **condensation** reactions. Examples are phenol formaldehyde (PF) and urea formaldehyde (UF), both of which find application as adhesives, particularly in industry. UF has an interesting application in "wet-strength" paper tissues and towels. The resin is incorporated in paper pulp during manufacture and forms a coating round each fibre. This prevents water saturating the hollow fibres but still allows absorption by capillary action.

condensation
polymerisation

The polymerisation of phenol formaldehyde can be considered as follows. Phenol, C_6H_5OH, has the structural formula:

Formaldehyde, HCHO, is represented by:

These two monomers can react in the following way:

Water is again given off during the condensation reaction. Similar reactions can occur between the formaldehyde molecule and other hydrogen atoms in the phenol molecule to give a three-dimensional network. The network can be depicted as:

The basic types of polymer and the way they are formed has been established. You can now consider some of the characteristics that determine how they are used, particularly in conservation work.

D Some important characteristics of polymeric materials

D1 Terminology

Of the vast numbers of chemical compounds that exist, a great many are polymers, and they range from the relatively simple synthetic materials like polythene and poly(vinyl acetate) and fairly straight-forward natural materials such as cellulose, to the complex compounds of proteins, DNA and beyond. All polymers can be considered in terms of the two types introduced in this chapter – *long-chain* and *network* polymers. However, a great deal of research and development on polymers has followed the commercial production of the first plastics products around the turn of the century, and this has led to the use of certain terms with which you need to be familiar — in particular *thermoplastics* and *thermosetting plastics* (or, simply, *thermosets*).

As its name implies, a **thermoplastic** is a material that becomes plastic, capable of being moulded, as it is heated. When these materials are warmed they become soft and can be formed into a desired shape. On cooling, they become rigid, but soften again on reheating. Thermoplastics consist of **long-chain polymers**, combined with various other molecules that modify their properties. A mass of long-chain polymer molecules is held together only by relatively weak secondary bonds between neighbouring molecules. Consequently, the molecules can be made to slide over one another relatively easily, particularly with increasing temperature. As you will see, the weak bonding between molecules influences many of the important properties of a thermoplastic.

A **thermosetting plastic** when fully polymerised, or *cured*, consists of a continuous network in which sliding between molecules cannot occur. In effect, the whole structure is one large molecule with all atoms linked by primary covalent bonds. The application of heat accelerates polymerisation and produces a permanent *set* of the material; hence the term **thermoset**.

In general, then, thermoplastics are based on long-chain polymers, and thermosets on network polymers. In conservation you will probably come across adhesives, coatings and consolidants based on natural as well as synthetic polymers, and so you may find it useful to consider this statement the other way round: materials consisting of long-chain polymers have the characteristics of thermoplastics, and network polymers behave like thermosets.

Once a thermoset is fully cured it *sets* irreversibly, and tends to be brittle and hard, and does not soften on heating; in fact, when heated it may char, burn or crumble. How is it then that thermosets can be used as, say, resins for fibreglass, for moulded articles such as electric light fittings, and as adhesives, coatings and consolidants? The answer is that when it is being worked, a thermoset is still a thermoplastic, that is, it consists of long-chain molecules that have not yet been joined together chemically. After the necessary shaping (moulding, brushing, spreading, and so on), the cross-linking process that produces the full polymer network is initiated. For thermosetting adhesives such as unsaturated polyesters and epoxys, this can be arranged very conveniently because the monomer that creates the cross-links can be kept separate until needed. Hence the two-pack boxes in which these materials are usually bought; one contains the pre-produced long-chain polymers, the other contains **hardener** (or **curing agent**) that produces the cross-links. Similarly, in the traditional paints that contain natural fatty oils, such as linseed oil, atmospheric oxygen forms the cross-links between the oil molecules to form the dried paint film.

At this point, it is appropriate to re-emphasise the distinction drawn earlier between polymers and plastics. Polymers are very

Marginal terms: **thermoplastic**, **long-chain polymers**, **thermosetting plastic**, **thermoset**, **hardener, curing agent**

large molecules made up by the successive linking together of one or more small molecules (monomers); plastics are a synthetic blend based on one or more types of polymer, usually with additions of other materials designed to produce desired changes in properties – to improve their flow properties, resistance to oxidation, ease of handling, colour and so on. Commercial adhesives, paints, lacquers and consolidants, are all examples of plastics. How some of these additions work will be discussed in the next section.

D2 Relating properties to structure

As a class, polymers provide a marvellous demonstration of how the properties of a material are determined by their internal structure. After all, combinations of atoms of only two elements, carbon and hydrogen, produce materials as different as methane, natural rubber and polystyrene; add another element, oxygen, and the variety of products seems endless, from the simple molecule of formaldehyde to polymethylmethacrylate, polyesters, cellulose, fats and many vitamins. This enormous range arises because the constituent atoms can be arranged in so many different ways. The internal structure of polymers can be conveniently classified at three different levels of scale:

1 The types of atom and the way they are held together in the molecules.

2 The size and shape of the molecule.

3 How the molecules are arranged relative to one another.

Before exploring these levels a little, and their inter-relation, in terms of their properties, two terms need to be defined: *crystalline* and *amorphous*. When the atoms or molecules in a solid form a regular three-dimensional array, that solid is said to be **crystalline**. In such an arrangement the atoms or molecules are in their most stable positions, so **crystallinity** is the normal condition of solids.

crystalline solids

crystallinity

Metals and alloys are aggregates of small crystals. Snowflakes are crystals, and so are diamonds, sapphires and rubies. When allowed to form without physical constraint (for instance, a snowflake), the internal order of a crystalline solid is manifested externally by its symmetrical plane faces. These regular geometric shapes are what we normally think of as crystals. However, it is the regular internal structure that defines crystallinity and not the outward appearance.

On the other hand, a solid in which the arrangement of atoms or molecules has no regular order over any appreciable distance is called **amorphous**; the wide variety of glasses and glazes are examples.

amorphous solids

Some polymers are completely amorphous, some are mainly amorphous with a few crystalline regions, and others have a significant degree of crystallinity. In some forms of polythene, for instance, more than half of the volume is crystalline. The degree of crystallinity in a polymer is an important factor in determining its properties, so it is useful to look in a bit more detail at why crystallinity can vary so much. Consider, for instance, what happens to a thermoplastic (a mass of long-chain molecules) as it is cooled from the molten (liquid) state.

As you will remember from Book 1, the liquid state is characterised by an arrangement of molecules which is highly disordered and therefore relatively less closely packed. As a consequence a liquid has a lower density than the equivalent solid, and also a lower viscosity, that is, the molecules occupy more space and, because they are less strongly bound, slide over one another more easily. (Water and ice are exceptions – there might be less frost damage if ice were denser than water.)

As the thermoplastic cools below its melting point, at which temperature the solid form becomes more stable than the liquid form, the molecules attempt to attain the ordered arrangement of a crystal. As you know from Books 1 and 2, the atoms or molecules in a material are in a constant state of motion due to the thermal (kinetic) energy they possess, and the higher the temperature the greater is the thermal energy. The regular arrangement of a crystal cannot occur instantaneously on cooling because it takes time for the atoms or molecules to move to an appropriate place in the ordered arrangement. In practice, crystalline regions begin to grow at various points (called nuclei, but not to be confused with atomic nuclei) in the liquid, and they grow into the liquid as further atoms or molecules move to join the regular array. The final result of this process would be a solid consisting of a mass of small crystals; a **polycrystalline aggregate**, as it is called. This is what happens in metals because the single atoms involved are sufficiently mobile to fit into a regular array. In polymers, however, the same configuration is rarely, if ever, attained. There are two reasons for this. First, long molecules have a very limited mobility in the liquid compared with single atoms. Second, even if they could move freely, the size and shape of the molecules often militates against *all* of the molecules lining up like sticks in a bundle. If bulky side-groups are attached at irregular points along the molecule, they are unlikely to pack together easily. For example, random co-polymers are less likely to crystallise than block co-polymers. On the other hand, strong secondary bonding between polymer molecules encourages the development of crystallinity.

polycrystalline aggregate

Figure 2.10 lists some of the common polymers that are either amorphous or significantly crystalline.

Crystalline
polyethylene (PE)
saturated polyesters
cellulose
cellulose acetate (CA)
polyamides (for example, nylons)

Amorphous
polymethylmethacrylate (PMMA) and co-polymers
PVAC-PE co-polymers
polystyrene (PS)
all thermosets

Figure 2.10 *Crystalline and amorphous polymers. (This is not a rigid classification as many factors can influence the degree of crystallinity.)*

Notice that the lists bear out the general points made above about molecule shape. Those that give rise to strong secondary forces between molecules due to polar side-groups, especially $C = O$, often take part in hydrogen-bonding (to —OH groups, for instance) and tend to have a degree of crystallinity; those with small regularly spaced side-groups behave similarly, but those with large side-groups are usually amorphous. Where there is an irregular structure but *no* polar side-groups the polymers tend to be "rubbery" (for example, natural rubber). To help you visualise the molecular arrangements in long-chain polymers, Figure 2.11 illustrates the type of model that has been used to describe an amorphous and a highly crystalline material.

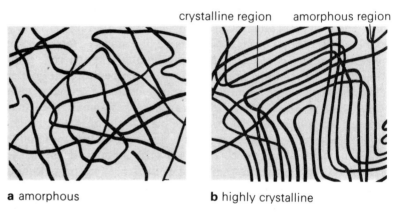

a amorphous   **b** highly crystalline

Figure 2.11 *Amorphous and crystalline polymer structures.*

Drawing a polymer out into a fibre increases its crystallinity – just as stretching a piece of cotton-wool aligns many of the fibres in the direction of pull. As Figure 2.11 illustrates, even a highly crystalline polymer contains amorphous regions.

From the above discussion of the problem of crystallisation it is clear that amorphous polymers have such awkward molecular structures and high viscosity that they do not crystallise at all. When cooled, they exhibit the properties of a solid, such as becoming more rigid and dense. Unlike crystalline materials, they do not show a sharp melting point as they change from solid to liquid on heating. In this way they are like glasses which alter gradually from being like a solid material to being like a liquid over a range of temperature. The lower limit of this temperature range is called the **glass transition temperature** (or, simply, **glass point**). The conventional symbol for it is T_g (sometimes t_g). Essentially, at this temperature the available thermal energy is small compared with the forces holding the molecules together. At lower temperatures, very little molecular adjustment is possible, in other words, the molecular structure is "frozen in". For example, below its glass transition temperature (T_g) an amorphous polymer is typically hard and brittle; above T_g it is typically softer and more rubber-like, is more readily permeated by gases and can be dissolved more easily.

glass transition temperature, (glass point)

Clearly, the glass transition temperature of a polymer is extremely relevant to the uses of the polymer. The values of T_g for many of the polymers referred to in this text are given in Figure 2.12. Notice that thermoplastics that are classed as crystalline also have a T_g because they, inevitably, contain amorphous regions.

You can see that in their raw state, materials such as cellulose acetate, polymethylmethacrylate and PVC are hard, brittle and glass-like at ordinary temperatures. However, long-chain polymers like these can be mixed with other chemicals which effectively decrease T_g; that is, they induce rubber-like properties, such as enhanced flow, at lower temperatures.

Polymer	T_g (°C)
polyethylene (PE)	−35 to −90
natural rubber	−75
nylon 6	50
polyvinyl chloride (PVC)	85
polystyrene (PS)	95
polymethylmethacrylate (PMMA)	105
cellulose acetate (CA)	105

Figure 2.12 *The approximate glass transition temperatures for some common polymers (rounded to the nearest 5°C).*

Such substances are called **plasticisers** and are relatively involatile solvents of the polymer. By being incorporated between the molecules of individual polymers and weakening the *inter*-molecular bonds, they separate the long chains and facilitate their movement relative to one another. Plasticisers need to behave like a solvent in order to carry out their function and they also need to have a low

plasticisers

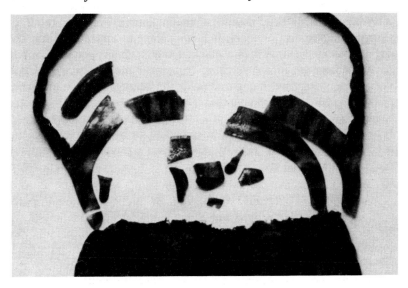

Figure 2.13 *The artificial horn clasp on this 1920s handbag shows embrittlement due to loss of camphor plasticiser from celluloid.*

vapour pressure — so that they do not evaporate, or do so only slowly. (They normally have a molecular mass greater than 300.) Clearly, the evaporation of a plasticiser leads to brittleness — an ageing problem often met in adhesives, coatings and consolidants. A few practical examples should help to emphasise the importance of a plasticiser. Cellulose nitrate is a hard brittle thermoplastic at ordinary temperatures; its T_g is similar to that of cellulose acetate, about 100°C. Mixing it with camphor as the plasticiser led to developments of the first plastic, namely Parkesine and, later, Celluloid.

PVC in its pure form is one of the hard, rigid plastics you come across in the clear plastic bottles used to contain fruit drinks. When plasticised, it becomes soft and pliable, and is used in "leathercloth" for bookbindings, car seats, gloves and so on. Common plasticisers for PVC are esters formed between ortho-phthalic acid:

COOH

COOH

and alcohols containing about eight carbon atoms.

Manipulating the formulation of a plastic can reach a high degree of subtlety. For instance, as you will see in Chapter 6, the glass transition temperature for an emulsion paint should lie, initially, some degrees below ordinary temperatures when the paint is being applied, so that a continuous paint film is obtained. Ultimately, however, the film may need to be hard and glasslike, that is, have a T_g above ordinary temperature. This is achieved by incorporating a small amount of fugitive (volatile) plasticiser in the thermoplastic polymer paint base. During the final stages of drying, this plasticiser is slowly lost by evaporation, thus producing a rise in T_g.

Finally, in this brief review of the structure–property relationship in long-chain polymers, it is important to appreciate that the degree of crystallinity has a marked effect on properties. This is basically because in a crystalline region the molecules are packed very closely together compared with the arrangement in an amorphous region. Which means that the spaces between molecules are smaller and the binding forces stronger. As a consequence, in general, a crystalline polymer is expected to have, for example, a higher strength and rigidity than the equivalent amorphous polymer, and to be less easily dissolved and less readily permeated by gases.

Of course, network polymers (thermosets) are very different to long-chain polymers (thermoplastics). By their very nature, they are amorphous, and since they consist of one continuous molecule, they do not undergo glass transition in the same way as thermoplastics. Their mechanical strength, rigidity and hardness are determined essentially by the spacing between the cross-links along the molecule: the more frequent the cross-links, the more rigid the material, and the more insoluble it becomes.

Making joints with different types of adhesive

A   Solvent adhesives

    A1   Cellulose nitrate

    A2   Poly (vinyl acetate)

B   Reaction adhesives

    B1   Epoxy adhesives

    B2   Cyanoacrylates ("superglues")

C   Melt-freeze adhesives

    C1   Soldering and brazing

    C2   Welding

    C3   Melt-freeze adhesives and the effects of heat

Making joints
with different types of adhesive

Now that some of the chemistry of polymers has been explained, it is possible to look in more detail at the range of adhesives which are available for joint-making. Since this book is not an adhesives manual, by no means all the individual adhesives will be covered, but the three classes of adhesives – which embrace all the materials used in conservation – will be discussed. They are solvent, reaction and melt-freeze adhesives.

A Solvent adhesives

"No one should use a solvent-based adhesive and nobody should make one. They contain only one-quarter to one-third of useful adhesive; they are inflammable, toxic, foul-smelling and expensive since you are going to throw over half the bulk away by evaporation. Solvent-adhesives are legislated against, one by one solvents are banned [. . . .]" (K. W. Harrison, *Adhesion*, Vol. 3, Applied Science Publishers, 1979)

In spite of these very appropriate thoughts, **solvent adhesives** are widely used in conservation and therefore warrant serious consideration in this text.

The principle on which solvent adhesives are based is simple: the adhesive is dissolved in a suitable solvent so that it can be applied to a surface in liquid form. The solvent then evaporates to leave the solid joint. The adhesive bonds so formed are mainly due to secondary forces between molecules in the adhesive and those of the surface. The considerable advantages of solvent adhesives in conservation work are that unlike melt-freeze adhesives they can be

solvent adhesives

made to spread very easily (because of very low viscosity), and, unlike reaction adhesives, the joints are more readily reversed. On the other hand, in addition to the disadvantages cited in the above quotation, perhaps their greatest shortcoming is the shrinkage and embrittlement that can occur during ageing owing primarily to the loss of solvent. Examples of solvent adhesives commonly used are cellulose nitrate, poly(vinyl acetate) and its co-polymers, hydrolysed starch and animal glues (various gelatins produced by the breakdown of collagen, a component of bone, cartilage and skin).

A1 Cellulose nitrate

Cellulose nitrate was one of the first synthetic polymers to be widely used. It was the first plastic base for ciné-film. Many early plastic objects and utensils were moulded using Celluloid, the commercial name which is most commonly associated with cellulose nitrate. In conservation its use stretches back more than fifty years and because of tradition and the acceptable results achieved, it is still used for many jointing purposes, notably archaeological pottery.

The polymerisation of glucose monomers to form long-chain molecules of cellulose was described on page 34 and it was shown that cellulose nitrate is formed by the reaction of nitric acid with some of the hydroxyl (—OH) side-groups of the cellulose molecule. Part of a cellulose molecule is illustrated in Figure 2.8; cellulose nitrate is similar but with about two-thirds of the hydroxyl side-groups replaced by nitrate (—NO$_3$) groups.

The solvents most commonly used in cellulose nitrate adhesives are mixtures of acetone, ethanol and butyl acetate. During its long use in conservation no unwanted side-effects have been observed, and, after many years, it is still found to be soluble and therefore the joints are reversible. There is something to be said for the old, well-tried and tested materials. However, it has three major drawbacks: brittleness and shrinkage, as well as the evolution of nitric acid when it breaks down.

The hydrogen-bonding between the —OH groups on neighbouring cellulose molecules is strong, and this is reduced in cellulose nitrate by the presence of the —NO$_3$ groups. Nevertheless, solid cellulose nitrate is a relatively rigid material, and is brittle. It is usually used without any additives, but can be made more flexible by the addition of a plasticiser that separates the molecules to some extent and enables them to slide over one another. Camphor is the plasticiser normally used. This helps to solve one problem but causes another. With age, the camphor slowly volatilises, which means that the joint becomes more brittle and also shrinks.

In common with other solvent adhesives, cellulose nitrate shrinks during setting because of the loss of solvent. The result of this is that joints made with cellulose nitrate are rather weak and brittle, but in many conservation applications, such as the repair of earthenware, they are quite satisfactory.

A2 Poly(vinyl acetate)

Poly(vinyl acetate) must be one of the most widely used adhesives and it has also found conservation applications in consolidation and coating. As an adhesive it has been used for support fabrics in textile conservation, for mending ceramics and in stone conservation for example. Like several classes of polymer (**acrylics**, polymers of acrylic acid: $CH_2 = CH$ (COOH), are another common example) poly(vinyl acetate) can be used as a solution or an emulsion. Its use as an adhesive will be discussed in these terms. Sometimes the properties of an organic solution will be preferred: at other times an aqueous emulsion will be more suitable for the job in hand. **acrylics**

Calling this material PVA for short, as is often done for commercial products, can be misleading because it is also used to describe poly(vinyl alcohol). It is better to call them PVAC and PVAL respectively. In its pure form PVAC forms a clear glassy solid with a high resistance to heat, light, dilute acids, dilute alkalies and water. It dissolves readily in many organic liquids, and acetone and ethanol are commonly used as solvents for the solution adhesive. Because PVAC is a thermoplastic of good chemical stability, joints made with it are easily reversed by dissolution. Like cellulose nitrate, it is fairly brittle, but a small amount of solvent is retained for a considerable time and acts as a plasticiser. (Blocks of PVAC dissolved in ethanol and left to harden have remained flexible for several years.)

A number of PVAC adhesives are available commercially (usually labelled "PVA adhesive") and recommended for use on wood, paper and fabrics. These materials are usually in the form of an **emulsion** or **dispersion**. An emulsion consists of finely dispersed particles of the adhesive polymer in suspension in water. The best known example of an emulsion is milk which consists of minute particles of fat in suspension in an aqueous medium. **emulsion**
dispersion

Demonstration

Pour some oil (cooking oil) and some water into a bottle and shake vigorously. You will notice that the oil breaks up into small droplets that are dispersed in the water. However, the droplets soon coalesce and the water and oil separate as two distinct layers; the same happens when cream floats to the top of a bottle of milk. Now add a small amount of washing-up liquid (or a soap solution) and you will find that the emulsion lasts for much longer. As you know from Book 2, soap molecules are *surfactants*; they have a hydrophobic (water-repelling) end and a hydrophilic (water-attracting) end. The soap molecules diffuse and collect on the oil droplets and act as a barrier that inhibits coalescence of the droplets. This is illustrated in Figure 3.1 (overleaf) in which soap molecules are represented by a convention which you will remember from Book 2.

Adhesive emulsions behave in a similar way to the mixture of oil, water and soap solution. As the water evaporates from the emulsion, the particles of polymer coalesce to form a continuous solid. To form an homogeneous solid the polymer molecules must be able to move

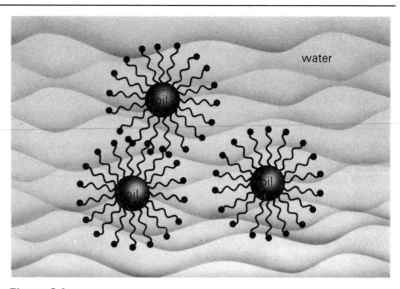

water

oil

oil

oil

Figure 3.1

and adjust their positions. This means that the polymer must be a thermoplastic and above its glass transition temperature, T_g. Of course, to make a good joint, the resultant solid needs to be rigid, and this requires the polymer to be below its T_g. As pointed out in Chapter 2, Section D2, this change is achieved by incorporating a small amount of plasticiser that evaporates as the adhesive dries out.

emulsion stabilisation

In the case of PVAC emulsion adhesives, the surfactant usually used to **stabilise** the emulsion (stop the polymer from settling out) is poly(vinyl alcohol) (PVAL), which with its —OH groups is hydrophilic. Some plasticiser is also added. The solids formed from aqueous emulsions are inevitably sensitive to moisture, due to the presence of the hydrophilic stabiliser, and this necessitates the addition of fungicide and bactericides – and restricts the use of PVAC emulsion adhesives to applications indoors.

Emulsions such as these are very useful because they allow much more control over the polymerisation process and, therefore, the properties of the adhesive. But, as usual, there are swings and roundabouts. The addition of these chemicals increases the susceptibility to oxidation and possibly the formation of cross-links and increasing insolubility of the adhesive. The *volatilisation* (vapourisation) of these chemicals, especially in the confined atmosphere of a display case, may also lead to corrosion of metal objects on display.

B Reaction adhesives

There are many instances where the use of solvent adhesives is unsuitable. This occurs most often because they set too slowly, shrink too much and do not give joints of sufficient strength. Although strength is not, for its own sake, important in conservation, it is necessary that the weight of a heavy ceramic or metal object will be supported by the joint. Dowelling with stainless steel rods may accomplish this in some cases but it is also often necessary to use **reaction adhesives**.

These adhesives are produced *in situ* by chemical reactions and adhesion is due mainly to strong secondary bonds. They are usually thermosetting (network) polymers and are formed by one of two main methods: one in which the cross-linking monomer and other chemicals to initiate and control the network formation are kept separate from long-chain polymers and mixed when required; and one in which polymerisation is inhibited until the monomer makes contact with the surfaces to be joined. Epoxy resins such as the Araldite family are examples of the former, and alkyl cyano-acrylates ("superglues") are examples of the latter.

Not all reaction adhesives are made from organic polymers. For instance, plaster of Paris, cement and mortar also solidfy *in situ* by means of chemical and physical reactions.

The starting materials for thermosetting adhesives may contain a small amount of liquid to aid their ease of spreading, but far less than for a solvent adhesive. This, in addition to the fact that the solid product is a rigid, yet still open, network polymer, means that as a consequence shrinkage of the solid joint is usually very small. The joint can be fairly firm ten or fifteen minutes after it has been formed, but it may be many hours before it is completely set. The rate of the cross-linking chemical reaction depends on temperature, and so the reaction is accelerated by warming the adhesive.

However, most of the polymerisation reactions in this type of adhesive are *exothermic* – they give out heat; the heat released accelerates the process. In selecting such an adhesive, consider whether the heat evolved could damage the object – by, for instance, causing evaporation of moisture and thus internal stresses.

reaction adhesives

B1 Epoxy adhesives

An epoxy resin adhesive (or epoxide adhesive) is made in two stages. The first step is to produce relatively long-chain molecules by condensation polymerisation reactions. Typical monomers in this reactions are shown in Figure 3.2. They are known by confusing non-systematic names, epichlorhydrin (3.2(a)) and Bis-phenol A (3.2(b)).

Figures 3.2

a *epichlorhydrin*

b *Bis-phenol A*

The initial reaction is, in effect, a condensation between these two molecules followed by further additions in which the three-membered ring in epichlorhydrin is opened to form an open chain

c

with a hydroxyl —OH group on it. The product of this reaction (3.2c) is the so-called resin component of a two-pack system.

In the second step – the one that is carried out *in situ* – these linear chains are cross-linked by addition polymerisation reactions using another monomer. The monomer in the cross-linking stage is usually a di- or polyamine, a compound containing two or more —NH₂ groups, such as diethylene triamine ($NH_2CH_2CH_2NHCH_2CH_2NH_2$). The cross-link is produced when the amine group reacts with two epoxy groups. The COC three-membered ring is called the epoxy **epoxides** group and compounds containing it are called **epoxides**.

d

Figure 3.2(d) shows the reaction of one end of a polyamine with the two epoxy end groups of the long-chain molecules. Similar reactions will take place at the other amine groups on the polyamine and this causes the build-up of a network.

Many different resins and hardeners can be used and the number of permutations of these is very large. A manufacturer often sells a wide range of different epoxy systems to cover all sorts of operating conditions; different temperatures, different setting times, different "spreadability", and even ones that will cure under water. Very few epoxy adhesives are completely colourless, and this may be a disadvantage, particularly on glass. Because of the nature of the production processes, colour and other properties may vary between batches, so it is important not to rely too heavily on the characteristics of one sample. Some of the starting materials deteriorate with time in their containers because the ingredients undergo chemical changes. These reactions can be inhibited by keeping the containers in a refrigerator – the lower the temperature, the slower is a chemical reaction (see Book 1, Chapter 2, and Book 2, Chapter 7).

To achieve maximum rigidity and strength of the adhesive, it is essential for the resin and hardener to be mixed in the recommended proportions. In fact, room-temperature curing does not achieve the full bonding potential of the adhesive. For the polymeric network of the thermoset to be developed, that is, for cross-links to be formed, the cross-linking agent has to be mobile and diffused through the resin. Thus the molecules of the resin must be able to move to accommodate the cross-linking monomer – it must be above its T_g. As more and more cross-links are formed, the material becomes more rigid and its T_g is effectively raised. Diffusion is therefore inhibited and the cross-linking reaction stops. Raising the temperature above T_g permits the reaction to resume. In industrial applications, curing is often carried out in two stages; the first at room temperature which produces partial curing sufficient to hold the pieces in place, and the second at a temperature that produces the required degree of cross-linking and thereby strength and stiffness.

Diffusion will be dealt with in a little more detail in Chapter 5.

Fully developed joints formed with epoxy adhesives are very strong, sometimes as strong as the parent material – even some metals. They are also insoluble in common solvents, so a joint is difficult to reverse. (Dichloromethane will, as a result of slow diffusion, eventually produce sufficient swelling to disrupt the solid. Nitromors paint stripper relies on this effect.)

B2 Cyanoacrylates (''superglues'')

These glues are a relatively new development and are already of considerable importance for domestic uses. They may also come to find significant applications in conservation work, but uncertainty about reversibility and their requirement for clean, well-fitting surfaces are definite limitations. One application already proposed is for tacking glass fragments quickly into position by the minimum number of spots of cyanoacrylate glue. Once the fragments are accurately in position, epoxy resin adhesive can be drawn into the break by capillary action to form the main adhesive joining the fragments together.

Cyanoacrylate adhesives are based on the alkyl–2–cyano-acrylate monomers of the form:

cyanoacrylate adhesives

In this structural formula, R represents the methyl ($-CH_3$), ethyl ($-C_2H_5$), or butyl ($-C_4H_9$) side-groups. When R is methyl, you will see that this monomer is very similar to methyl methacrylate (which polymerises to form polymethylmethacrylate, Perspex or Plexiglas). The only difference is that the cyanoacrylate has a cyano ($-C \equiv N$) side-group instead of the methyl linked to the carbon backbone.

The adhesive is usually supplied in a container as a monomer combined with an acid that prevents the polymerisation reaction. If the acid is neutralised, then the monomer polymerises and becomes solid. The hydroxyl ($-OH$) groups found on most surfaces in the presence of water will neutralise the acid. On applying the monomer to a surface, the acid is removed and curing starts. If there are too few hydroxyl groups present a solid joint will not be formed. This will occur, for instance, if the surfaces are acidic, as happens with wood since this releases acetic acid, or if the atmosphere is too dry.

The smaller the R side-group, the stronger and stiffer the joint, and they are the strongest so far produced with an organic adhesive. The larger the R side-group, the slower is the curing time. Since the methyl monomer cures very rapidly it may be preferable to use the butyl monomer if the assembled parts have to be aligned after contact. Although a strong bond is formed in a few seconds, complete curing takes a few hours, and during this time the joint can be removed using acetone.

Since these adhesives have only been produced for a few years, little is yet known about their ageing characteristics, so they should be used with caution.

C Melt-freeze adhesives

Although the vast majority of adhesives used in conservation fall into the two categories already discussed, there are times where neither solvent nor reaction adhesives are suitable. In those cases **melt-freeze adhesives** better results may be achieved by **melt-freeze adhesives**.

A melt-freeze adhesive is a material that is melted to allow a joint to be made whilst the adhesive is liquid; on cooling the adhesive re-solidifies. By definition, therefore, it has to be a thermoplastic. These materials provide the most rapid way of making a completed joint because they do not involve evaporation of solvent or a chemical curing reaction.

Naturally-occurring organic materials have been used as melt-freeze adhesives in conservation work for many centuries; examples are rosin (colophony), shellac and beeswax. In ancient times sealing wax was made from beeswax, and in the last two centuries or so it has been made from a mixture of shellac and rosin mixed with turpentine or oil, and pigment. The turpentine is added as a plasticiser to increase the toughness; with age the turpentine diffuses out and evaporates and the wax becomes brittle. Synthetic waxes produced as by-products of the distillation of coal or refining of crude oil, are also used; examples are paraffin wax (a hydro-carbon) and microcrystalline wax (a branched hydrocarbon) that find application in the lining and impregnation of paintings.

Other advantages of the materials cited are that they melt at relatively low temperatures — and are therefore not likely to induce thermal damage in most objects — and they are relatively stable chemically. However, because the polymer molecules have few if any reactive (polar) side-groups, their adhesive and cohesive bonding is relatively weak. In addition, when molten they have a high viscosity and so they are difficult to spread.

In recent years a number of improved wax formulations have been developed, mainly because of the use of waxed paper for wrapping bread, and of waxed cartons for milk, and so on. These developments provide a good example of how knowledge of the internal structure of a material can suggest alterations which will improve its properties. Paraffin wax and, as its name implies, microcrystalline wax are crystalline thermoplastics consisting of long hydrocarbon molecules. With no polar side-groups, inter-molecular bonding is very weak and so the solid waxes are very soft. One way of improving the strength without affecting adversely other properties would be to add polythene, which itself is very similar to paraffin wax but with extremely long molecules. Unfor-tunately, it is not easily soluble in the waxes because of its crystal-linity. However, ethylene-vinyl acetate co-polymers (known as EVA) *are* soluble. The EVAs are *random* co-polymers and essentially amorphous. As a result they are more compatible with paraffin and other waxes. A bonus obtained from such compositions is that the polar $C = O$ side-groups contributed by vinyl acetate increase the adhesive bonding potential.

Another reason for describing how these materials work is that somewhat similar adhesives have been developed for use in con-servation (particularly of paintings), specifically the Beva series of adhesives. They are actually a variant of melt-freeze adhesives and are called **heat-seal adhesives**. The basic idea behind this type of adhesive is to use a long-chain polymer (an ethylene-vinyl acetate co-polymer) for structural strength together with short-chain polymers (usually hydrocarbon resins) with a melting point in the range 80–100°C. On heating, the resin melts to form a runny (low viscosity) liquid in which the co-polymer dissolves. It is used in this condition and on cooling reverts to a solid mass. In conjunction with hydrocarbon solvents such as toluene, these materials can be used as consolidants and coatings*.

heat-seal adhesives

Not all melt-freeze adhesives need be polymers. For a great many years melt-freeze adhesives have been used to join pieces of metal

---

* For more information on these important new adhesives see, for example, G. A. Berger, 'Formulating adhesives for the conservation of paintings', in **Conservation and Restoration of Pictorial Art**, Brommelle and Smith (eds.), Butterworths/IIC, London 1976, pp. 169–81.

by the techniques known as *soldering, brazing* and *welding*. In these instances the adhesive is a metal alloy which, in principle, behaves in a similar fashion to organic melt-freeze adhesives.

Soldering, brazing and welding are widespread metal-working techniques and the science of joining by these means has significant implications for conservators. Soldering and brazing are similar in principle, so these will be considered before welding, which has some considerable differences.

C1 Soldering and brazing

Both of these processes are similar to the melt-freeze waxes that have just been discussed, in that pieces of a (metal) object are joined by an adhesive that has a lower melting point than the pieces to be joined. The main difference between soldering and brazing lies in the composition, and particularly the consequent melting points, of the adhesives that are used. Soldering generally refers to joining at lower temperatures than brazing.

soldering   In **soldering**, the adhesive (the solder), in the form of a wire, is melted (using a soldering iron) and then allowed to spread over the surfaces to be joined. The liquid solder interacts with the surfaces of the metal pieces to be joined and forms a very thin adhesive layer of *alloy*. Figure 3.3 shows, schematically, how the adhesive bond is produced. The solder itself is a metal alloy, and bonding occurs as a result of the intermingling of atoms that occurs across the interface between the solder and the metal object.

Random atomic movement is occurring rapidly in the hot liquid solder, but there is virtually no movement in the cold solid or interchange of atoms between the two materials. As thermal energy is transferred from the molten solder to the solid metal, the metal object warms up and so movement of atoms between it and the solder becomes easier. When the source of heat is removed, the solder cools and solidifies, and the resulting arrangement of atoms at the interface is depicted in Figure 3.3(b). Some of the atoms in the solder will have moved (diffused) into the metal object, and vice versa. Since the atoms in the solder and in the metal object are held together by primary metallic bonds, there is a continuity of primary bonding across the interface. Thus, in soldered joints, the major means of adhesion is primary chemical bonding. Although atoms from the solder only penetrate the object for a seemingly short distance, (typically a quarter of a millimetre), a soldered joint is stronger than those obtained with solvent-adhesives and about as strong as those made with reaction-adhesives. Furthermore, solder

ductile   is a **ductile** alloy, that is it can be plastically deformed. Consequently soldered joints are *tough* (see Chapter 4, Section A) which means that they are usually more robust and able to stand harder knocks than organic adhesives.

The most familiar solders are made from alloys of tin and lead, and they melt at quite low temperatures, typically in the range 180–200°C. They are used on low melting metals such as pewter or where higher temperatures would damage the object (if lead solder

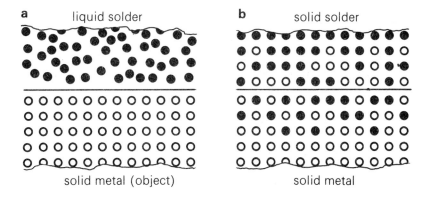

a liquid solder

b solid solder

solid metal (object)

solid metal

Figure 3.3 *This shows the stage at which the molten solder first contacts the solid, cold surface of the object.*

is already present on silver, high temperatures will cause total disintegration) or decoration (gilding, enamel, and so on).

Brazing is a similar process to soldering, indeed the two terms are not mutually exclusive. A convention that could be used is that soldering is performed at temperatures below 300°C, brazing at temperatures above 450°C. Traditionally, brazing alloys are commonly split into two classes, high-temperature **brazing** and low-temperature **brazing**. Low-temperature brazing is often called silver soldering or hard soldering. The brazing alloys are based on the silver–copper system with various other additions, and have melting points in the range 600–900°C. They are commonly used for articles made of silver. High-temperature brazing is a particularly good joining method for brasses (alloys of copper and zinc), and bronzes (alloys of copper and tin) and can also be used for cast-iron and wrought-iron. The brazing alloys used are based on the copper–zinc system with a melting range of about 850–900°C.

In both soldering and brazing, the joining alloy can be melted at a point on the joint and is drawn into the joint by capillary action. In the light of what has been said in Chapter 1, you will appreciate that for capillary action to work effectively, an adhesive must wet the surfaces of the object to be joined. Since both the adhesive (solder or brazing alloy) and the surfaces to be joined are metallic, it may be supposed that there would be no problem in the molten alloy wetting the object. This is not the case however because, for most metals, the surfaces to be joined will not be clean: they are usually tarnished in some way. In general, because they are not particularly stable chemically, metals react with chemicals in the atmosphere. The predominant reaction is with atmospheric oxygen, which produces a layer of oxide on the surface of the metal. When heat is applied the rate of this chemical reaction increases, and the

brazing

flux   resultant surface film stops the molten adhesive wetting the metal and therefore causes a weak joint to be formed; the molten adhesive does not penetrate the joint, and the surface film inhibits the formation of an adhesive bond. For this reason, the oxides and other contaminants have to be removed, and this is done by using a special substance, called a **flux**, in conjunction with the adhesive.

A flux is a material which, when molten, wets the tarnished metal and reacts chemically with the oxide or other contaminant to lay bare the clean underlying metal surface. The flux and the products of its reactions do not remain in the joint once the molten adhesive is introduced because they are much less dense and therefore float on the molten adhesive. Clearly, these features, plus the need for the flux to be molten at the soldering or brazing temperature, put stringent requirements on the choice of material for a flux.

Brazed joints are several times stronger than soldered joints and, when used on silver or copper alloys, of a strength comparable with that of the original metal.

The relative strengths of different metal-joining techniques can dictate which is used in a particular case in conservation. For example, the handles of pewter and silver jugs and cups tend to come away from the main body of the object after many years of constant use. These may be re-attached by an organic adhesive, but the adhesive bond achieved may not be sufficient for the object to be lifted repeatedly by the handles alone, and the joint will probably fail. However, a lead–solder joint on a pewter object, or a silver–solder (brazed) joint on a silver object, should be sufficiently strong so that the handles will not come away from the object when supporting the whole of its weight. For strong joints in objects made of iron alloys, or higher melting-point metals, an even higher temperature process, welding, must be used.

C2 Welding

welding   There are two types of **welding** process; those that involve a combination of *pressure* and usually heat, but not sufficient to cause melting; and *fusion* welding which relies on partially melting the pieces to be joined, usually in conjunction with a filler *metal*. Welding is not exclusive to metals. For instance, many plastics can be joined by pressing them together when warm; the seams in polythene bags are formed in this way. Broken candles or wax seals can be repaired by melting the wax in the vicinity of the crack with a heated spatula. In both of these examples, adhesion is achieved by diffusion across the joint interface, and usually the original interface is completely removed.

hammer-forging   An important example of welding under pressure and heat is the process known as **hammer-forging** practised by blacksmiths. Here, two pieces of metal are welded by heating them and hammering them together while they are still hot. Some metals will weld even without heat being applied. Two clean flat pieces of lead, gold or silver can be joined by simply hammering them cold. Again, the original interface disappears.

In **fusion welding**, the joint is heated intensely and locally, usually using a gas torch or an electric arc, and the join is formed by melting of the two surfaces, together with the "filler" metal (if one is being used) to fill the gap between the pieces. It is similar to soldering and brazing in that the adhesive bond is due to the primary metallic bonding produced between the pieces as a result of interdiffusion. The original interface disappears, see Figure 3.4.

fusion welding

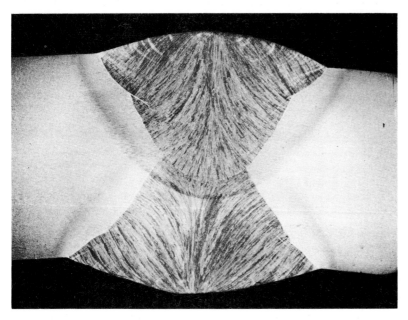

Figure 3.4 *Photomicrograph of a fusion welded joint, showing the interdiffusion between the filler metal and the metal being joined.*

Because of the very high local temperature involved, up to 3000°C, fusion welding is much more difficult to control than soldering and brazing. The major problem is rapid oxidation of the parent metal. This and other technical demands of the process have led to the development of a variety of techniques, but it is not appropriate to discuss them here.

Welded joints are very strong, and when well made are as strong as the parent metal. However, welding raises some problems when it is used in conservation. The most important one is that the melting of an alloy can lead to compositional changes; an important example of this is the *dezincification* of brass in which zinc is lost from the alloy because it is a relatively volatile element.

Perhaps the most serious problem arises from the **heat-affected zone** that is produced in an object that has been welded (see Figure 3.5). This is the volume of material around the site of a weld in which the constitution and character of the material is irreversibly changed. Typically, it can extend up to one centimetre from the region which was melted. It is not appropriate in this text to discuss in any detail the nature of the changes that can occur in the heat-affected zone, but you should know why such a zone is important.

heat-affected zone

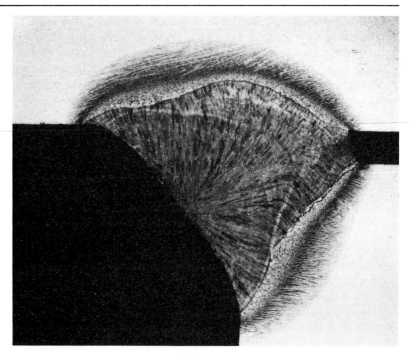

Figure 3.5 *Cracking in the heat-affected zone of a steel caused by hydrogen, as seen in the polished and etched section of a fillet-weld.*

Examples of how the arrangement of atoms or molecules in a material determine the properties of that material have already been considered. In most materials this relationship between structure and properties is complex. This is particularly so for metallic alloys because they usually consist of an aggregate of different compounds, and the sorts of compounds present, and their size and distribution, can be changed radically by thermal and mechanical treatments. Figure 3.6 illustrates this point for two samples of a low-carbon steel (iron with 0.4 per cent carbon). These photomicrographs were taken after the samples had been carefully polished and then etched in a chemical which attacks some constituents more rapidly than others. The white areas are virtually pure iron, and the dark areas consist of the compound iron carbide (Fe_3C).

Microstructures such as these can be analysed to determine the source of the material and the various mechanical and heat treatments it has undergone. In other words, by studying its microstructure, you can deduce the technology used to produce an object made of metal. In the heat-affected zone of a weld this information is destroyed; it is analogous to wiping and re-recording on a pre-recorded tape in a cassette deck.

Before leaving the subject of soldering, brazing and welding, some other effects of heat on materials should be mentioned. These can be significant in conservation work and can arise when using melt-freeze adhesives.

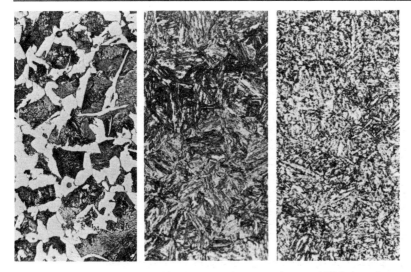

Figure 3.6 *Photomicrographs (at magnification of around 500 times) of three samples of the same low-carbon steel:* **a** *air cooled from 970°C,* **b** *quenched in water from 970°C,* **c** *water quenched from 970°C, tempered at 570°C for two hours.*

C3 Melt-freeze adhesives and the effects of heat

The application of heat, no matter how small the temperature rise it produces, can cause problems. Even the heat from an organic wax that melts at about 100°C can lead to some objects losing moisture, or to internal stresses that could be deleterious to fragile objects. Of course, at the higher temperature involved in soldering and brazing, and especially welding, the internal stresses are more severe.

Fortunately, many of the metals used in the objects that a conservator would meet are usually sufficiently ductile to withstand these stresses. However, fusion welding can embrittle an object through the absorption of chemicals from the environment. Such damage in a weld was shown in Figure 3.5 and this crack is the result of diffusion of hydrogen (from moisture or the gas used in the welding process) into the material.

The internal stresses set up by the rapid heating and cooling of a metal object that has a coating (such as enamel or a corrosion crust) can lead to damage. For a given rise in temperature, the thermal expansion of metals is considerably greater than that of other inorganic compounds such as oxides, carbonates, and so on, which constitute typical coatings. Also, such compounds are usually brittle. Thus when a metal with a coating is heated, the metal expands more than the coating which means that the metal exerts a pull on it. A tensile stress is set up in the coating, which may break and spall off in flakes. For this reason it is inadvisable to use soldering, brazing or welding on metal objects that are coated in this way. Apart from this problem the increase in temperature may produce colour changes in a patina, for instance in those found on old bronze.

The strength and stiffness
of materials

The strength and stiffness of materials

From Chapter 1, it is clear that the strength of a joint depends very much on the bonding at the interfaces between the adhesive and the broken surfaces of the object. This depends on the magnitude of the secondary forces between the adhesive and the object and on the potential number of bonding points. But there can be complications: if the coating of adhesive is too thick, the strength of the joint depends on the strength of the solid adhesive itself rather than on the interfaces. The coating has to be extremely thin, just a few molecular layers, before the bulk strength of the adhesive can be ignored.

From a practical point of view, the strength of the joint will be enhanced by a very close fit of the broken pieces. This enables the chemical bonding and mechanical keying to be at a maximum and reduces the effect of the bulk strength of the adhesive to a minimum.

Another important characteristic of a joint which is related to strength but, as you will see, utterly different from it, is its stiffness – or conversely, its floppiness. A joint between pieces of metals, glass or pottery, for instance, needs to be stiff and ideally as stiff as the object itself; joints in paper, leather or textiles, on the other hand, should be as flexible as the parent materials. There are of course cases where a flexible joint is an advantage with a stiff material, for example, adhesives which have flexibility could allow mended stained-glass in buildings to flex in strong winds.

The words "strength" and "stiffness", together with other words we associate with the response of something when it is pushed or pulled, or knocked or put under pressure, such as "force", "stress", "strain", "brittle" and "tough", are part of everyday vocabulary: "They face a very *stiff* task, and I'm not sure that they can both cope with the *stress*. Although she's quite *strong* and *tough* and doesn't show the *strain*, he's much more *brittle*, and I wouldn't want to *force* him in any way!"

However, scientific models that explain how materials respond when subjected to loads require strict definition of each of these words, and in order to understand the behaviour of an adhesive in these terms, you need to be clear about their precise meanings. This is the subject of the next three sections.

A Stress and strength

Any push or pull exerted on an object is an example of a *force*. Engines create forces that drive things, you create a force on a glass when you lift it to drink or on a car when you have to push it, and **tensile force** so on. A pulling force is called a **tensile force** and a pushing force **compressive force** a **compressive force**. The *weight* of an object also produces a force on the surface upon which it rests.

Look at Figure 4.1. Given that the glued joints are between the same materials, use the same adhesive, and that the joints are made equally well, it is obvious that a greater tensile force would be needed to break the joint in (a) than that in (b). Since the area of the interfaces between the object and the adhesive is greater in (a), there are more adhesive bonds across the joint and, therefore, a greater force would be needed to break them.

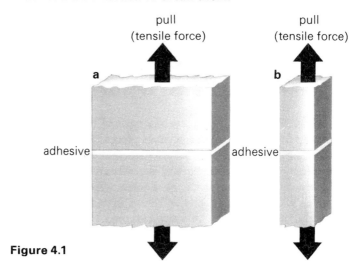

Figure 4.1

If you simply measured the strength of a joint as the force needed **breaking load** to break it (the **breaking load**), the result would only tell us something about that particular joint. Because the *size* of the joint is important, the result would not give any information on, for instance, the strength of the bond between adhesive and object, or the strength of the cohesive bonds within the adhesive itself or within the material being joined. To get this information the effect of size needs to be eliminated from the measurement of the breaking load.

Picture two rods of the same material where the cross-sectional area of one is *double* that of the other. If the two rods are pulled in tension, the thicker rod will support *double* the load that the thinner rod can take before it breaks. This was recognised a long time ago (by Galileo in fact) but it was not appreciated until very much later that if you divide the load needed to break a rod by its cross-sectional area, you get the same answer for rods of the same material no matter how thick they are. By doing this calculation, the effect of size is eliminated. The load on a piece of material divided by its cross-sectional area is called the **stress** in the material. When an **stress** object, such as a rod, of a particular material breaks, the stress acting in it is the same irrespective of its cross-sectional area and it is this stress that is called the **strength** of the material. Now look at this idea **strength** more formally.

Figure 4.2 represents a piece of material under tension. Imagine a cut made through it at right-angles to the tensile force to reveal a cross-section, the shaded area in Figure 4.2(a).

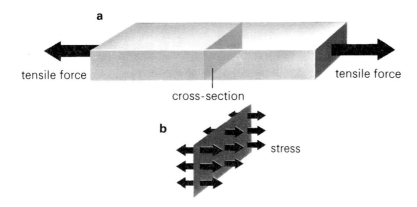

Figure 4.2

You can suppose that the tensile force is spread evenly over the whole of this cross-section. The stress is then calculated simply by dividing the force acting on the material by the cross-sectional area:

$$\text{stress} = \frac{\text{force}}{\text{area}}$$

The stress acting on the cross-section is illustrated in Figure 4.2(b).

The same situation would occur for any and every cross-section. Notice that the stress acts in opposing directions because in order to put a load on the material it has to be pulled at each end. The stress created by a tensile force is called a **tensile stress** and that created **tensile stress** by a compressive force, a **compressive stress**. **compressive stress**

Since stress acts at all points on a cross-sectional area of an object, it is basically a measure of the force by which the atoms or molecules

ultimate tensile strength

tensile strength

ultimate compressive strength

in the material are being pulled apart or pushed together. Consequently when the tensile or compressive force on a material reaches the stress at which some of its internal bonds are broken, the material begins to break. The maximum tensile stress a material can support before breaking is called the **ultimate tensile strength** (UTS) of the material; you will frequently see it referred to simply as **tensile strength**. Similarly, the maximum stress a piece of material can sustain in compression without breaking is called the **ultimate compressive strength**. (As you will see in Section 4C these definitions need to be modified slightly for materials that flow under load.)

Measurements of tensile strength provide a useful way of comparing different materials. Such measurements are made in specially designed tensile-testing machines, using standardised sizes and shapes of testpieces. Figure 4.3 shows the approximate tensile strength of a range of materials.

Material	General classification	Approximate value of tensile strength (MNm^{-2})
timber (across grain)		5
house brick		5
cement and concrete	extremely weak	5
stone		5–30
tanned leather		40
window glass		30–50
epoxy resin	weak	50
phenol formaldehyde		50
hard paste porcelain		70
fresh bone		100
timber (along grain)		100
copper	fairly strong	140
cast iron		70–140
wrought iron		100–300
human hair		200
silk fibre		350
catgut		350
mild steel	strong	400
copper alloys (for example bronzes and brasses)		100–600
nylon thread		1000
high-tensile steel wire (for example piano wire)	extremely strong	2000

Figure 4.3 *The approximate tensile strengths of a range of materials.*

The symbol MNm^{-2} in Figure 4.3 stands for mega-newtons per square metre* which is the internationally recognised unit for stress. If it is unfamiliar to you, don't worry, as all you have to do is compare one figure with another.

You can see that there is an enormous variation in the tensile strengths of different materials. This variation reflects the types of bonding and internal structural arrangements that occur in materials. For instance, note the huge difference in tensile strength for timber across and along the grain. Timber is a fibrous material, and has a grain, because long molecules of cellulose are packed very closely together in bundles; the bundles resemble drinking straws packed in a box. Now there is far less contact, and therefore less bonding, between molecules in neighbouring bundles than there is between molecules within a bundle. (This is also true of the molecules in drinking straws). So it is not surprising that timber is much stronger when pulled along the grain.

There is a very important caution about the data in Figure 4.3. The data are for typical samples of a given material that have been prepared under controlled conditions and of standardised shape and size. Other samples tested in other conditions could give values somewhat different from those quoted and this is particularly likely with the objects you handle. Most of the properties of a material, especially tensile strength, are not immutable. The internal constitution of a material depends on its history – how it was produced and subsequently treated. A sample with cracks or holes in it will have a lower tensile strength than normal (see Section 4D), similarly so would those that have corroded, rotted or been degraded in some way. However, bearing these limitations in mind, such data can be useful. For instance, notice that the widely used adhesives epoxy resin and phenol formaldehyde have a much lower tensile strength when solid than metals, but that they are stronger than wood tested across the grain. This raises the possibility that a joint made between pieces of wood with one of these adhesives could break within the wood rather than in the joint.

The units of stress. **The Système Internationale (SI)** *unit of force is the* **newton** *(N); 1 N is about the weight of an apple. The SI unit of area is the square metre* (m^2)*. So, stress (force/area) is measured in* **newtons per square metre** *$(N/m^2$ or $Nm^{-2})$. Officially in the SI system stress is measured in* **pascals** *(Pa), where 1 Pa = 1 Nm^{-2}, but the pascal has not proved to be popular, although you may meet it in some research literature. Since one newton is such a small force and the square metre is a large area, stress is often given in* **mega** *(million) newtons per square metre (MNm^{-2}). Unfortunately, a number of different systems of unit are in use today. The SI system is the official system in the scientific world and slowly making headway elsewhere. When you encounter other units for measuring stress, you may find the following conversions useful:*

$1\ MNm^{-2}\ = 10.2\ kgf\ cm^{-2}$ (kilogram force per square centimetre)

$\quad\quad\quad\quad\ = 146\ psi$ (pounds per square inch)

$1\ psi\quad\quad = 0.00685\ MNm^{-2} = 0.07\ kgf\ cm^{-2}$

$1\ kgf\ cm^{-2} = 0.098\ MNm^{-2}\quad = 14.2\ psi$

B Strain and stiffness

All solids change their shape (deform) when subjected to a weight or any other kind of force. When you stretch a rubber band or squeeze an eraser, the change of shape is obvious. If you try to squeeze a piece of glass, pottery, metal or wood between your fingers you will not detect a change of shape because a much greater force is needed in order to produce an observable change. These materials appear to have a greater *intrinsic* stiffness. When large objects made from these stiff materials are subject to large forces the deformation *is* observable; trees sway in the wind, aeroplane wings flap, and the tops of tall skyscrapers move a metre or two in a gale.

stiffness   It is clear that some objects are **stiffer** than others, that is, they are more resistant than others to changing their shape under an applied force. A branch is stiffer than a twig; they have the same intrinsic stiffness (they are made of the same material) but differ in dimensions. You have to get rid of the effects of geometry to look at the material alone in order to study these phenomena in a scientific way. To understand why some materials are intrinsically stiffer than others you need to consider the bonds that hold atoms and molecules together in a solid. Envisage that the millions of bonds between atoms or molecules in a material behave like minute springs. When a material is stretched or compressed each of these bonds is stretched or compressed too, and the overall change of shape of the material is the result of the many very small changes at a microscopic level. The effect produced in the spring-like bonds in a material is illustrated in Figure 4.4. Figure 4.4(a) represents the material when no force is being applied to it, (b) is the material under the tensile force indicated by the arrows, and (c) is the material under compression.

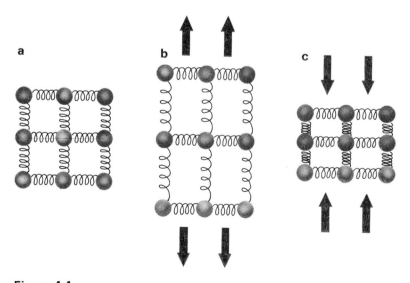

Figure 4.4

The intrinsic stiffness of a material is a measure of how much the atoms or molecules in a material *resist* being pulled apart or pushed together by an applied force; the stiffer the inter-atomic "springs", the stiffer is the material. To obtain a more precise definition of the stiffness of a material, a way of measuring the amount of deformation (change of shape) produced is needed that is independent of the size of an object. The answer lies in the concept of **strain**.

strain

Demonstration

Find a reasonably "stretchy" elastic band and put marks on it 2 and 4 cm apart. Then stretch the rubber band along a ruler. Figure 4.5 shows what happens.

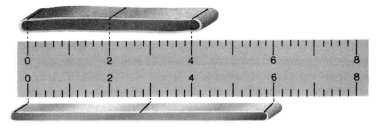

Figure 4.5

You will find that the 4 cm length has stretched to twice as long as the 2 cm length. The rubber band has been stretched uniformly along its length. You can check this for yourself by putting lots of marks close together on the strip and observing what happens when the band is stretched. If the *change* in length is divided by the *original length* the degree of stretch is found to be the same for both the 2 cm length *and* the 4 cm length. It is called the *strain*. Expressing it as a formula gives:

$$\text{strain} = \frac{\text{change in length}}{\text{original length}} = \frac{\text{new length minus original length}}{\text{original length}}$$

Check that the strain in your 2 cm and 4 cm lengths is the same. In the example shown in Figure 4.5, the 4 cm length stretched to 6 cm, and the 2 cm length to 3 cm.

For the 2 cm length, strain $= (3 \text{ cm} - 2 \text{ cm})/2 \text{ cm} = 1/2$ and for the 4 cm length, strain $= (6 \text{ cm} - 4 \text{ cm})/4 \text{ cm} = 2 \text{ cm}/4 \text{ cm} = 1/2$. Strain is sometimes expressed as a percentage; for instance, an extension of 1 mm in an original length of 100 mm may be expressed as either 0.01 or 1%. In the above example, the strain in the rubber band is $\frac{1}{2}$ or 50%.

When an eraser is squeezed or trees and skyscrapers sway, the strain produced in each case is *reversible*. On letting go, the eraser returns to its original shape, and the tree and skyscraper return to their upright position when the wind stops blowing. This *reversible* deformation is called **elastic deformation**, as opposed to the permanent, irreversible (**plastic**) **deformation** that can be produced in some materials.

elastic and plastic deformation

The stiffness of the material is the resistance it offers to being deformed *elastically*, and its stiffness can be measured as the *stress* needed to produce a specified amount of *elastic* strain. Notice that it is being defined in terms of stress and strain; that is, the size of the sample has been taken into account and so the result is a direct measure of an intrinsic property of the material concerned.

The stiffness of a material is given by dividing the stress by the strain:

$$\text{stiffness} = \frac{\text{stress}}{\text{strain}}$$

From this expression you can see that for a certain stress, the greater the amount of strain produced (the greater the percentage deformation) the less stiff is the material.

elastic modulus

Formally, the stiffness of a material is called the **elastic modulus** (the word "modulus" is derived from the Latin for "a measure"). For a given material there are several different elastic moduli, depending how the load is applied. So far we have only looked at tensile and compressive loads; for these cases the elastic modulus is called

Young's modulus

Young's modulus. Figure 4.6 shows approximate values for Young's modulus for a number of materials.

The units for measuring Young's modulus are the same as those for stress, for example, MNm^{-2}. This is because strain is just a number (it has no units), so dividing stress by strain alters the value but not the units.

Material	General classification	Young's modulus (MNm^{-2})
natural rubber	very flexible	7
polythene	fairly flexible	200
wood (across grain)		500
epoxy resin	rigid	4500
phenol formaldehyde		7000
wood (along grain)	very rigid	10,000–15,000
glass		70,000
stone		10,000–80,000
brasses and bronzes (copper alloys)		70,000
iron and steel		200,000
diamond	extremely rigid	1,200,000

Figure 4.6 *Approximate Young's Modulus values for a range of materials.*

Looking at the values from rubber to diamond, it is not surprising that you cannot squeeze a piece of pottery or glass between your fingers as you can a rubber. Notice also, that epoxy resin and phenol formaldehyde have a much lower Young's modulus than metals, glass, stone and wood along the grain; so, they would make glued joints with these materials that are more flexible than the adherends.

It is important to remember that, just as different metals have different values of Young's modulus, so will different formulations of epoxy resin. It is possible for you to adjust the physical properties of a resin, as will be seen later.

In many instances the forces which act on a joint will not be those of compression or tension. The example of appliqué art, where wood, metal or glass, say, are stuck to a vertical surface, would be a case where different forces operate. This different system of loading has already been met in Chapter 1C when you parted two wetted glass slides by sliding one over the other. In this case you would be applying **shear forces**. These are forces that attempt to produce a sliding motion. Tensile forces acting on an object have a common line of action, and so have compressive forces. On the other hand shear forces have parallel lines of action; look back at Figure 1.3 and check the alignment of the arrows that indicate the directions of the forces. You can see the different types of deformation (shape change) produced by the two types of force if you looked at the hypothetical joint in Figure 4.7(a). Assume that the joint is weakest at an interface between the adherend and the adhesive. Under a tensile force the joint will pull apart at the interface, Figure 4.7(b), and under a shear force, the joint is broken by sliding apart, Figure 4.7(c).

shear force

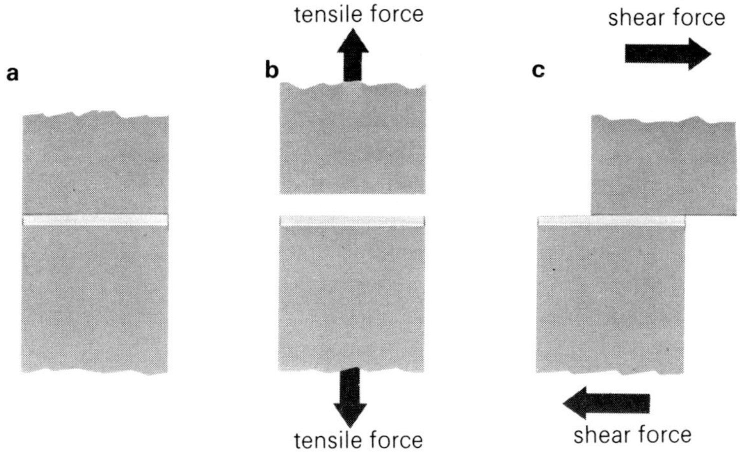

Figure 4.7 *A hypothetical joint subjected to tensile and sheer forces.*

One reason why shear forces are important is that in many materials the force needed to make atoms or molecules slide over one another is less than that needed to pull them apart. This provides the possibility of *plastic deformation* in which a material undergoes a *permanent* change of shape. It is a characteristic of most metals and of thermoplastics and glasses above their glass transition temperature. This phenomenon is looked at in more detail in the next section.

In practice, many objects are subjected to forces which are neither pure tension nor pure compression, but combinations of the two. Bending, the most important example of this, arises when a tensile or compressive load is applied to an object at a point a distance away from the points at which the object is supported. A floor joist spans the walls in a house and when you stand on it, it bends; when you lift a saucepan by the handle, the weight of the contents is acting at a distance from your hand, so the handle bends, and so on. You could determine the type of deformation produced in bending, using a piece of modelling clay (Plasticene) or an eraser.

Demonstration

Scratch a grid of lines on the face of a chunk of modelling clay (Plasticene) or an eraser, as illustrated in Figure 4.8(a), and then bend the eraser. You should get a result like that sketched in Figure 4.8(b), which is somewhat exaggerated to underline the effect. The top surface is stretched (the distance between scratches has been increased) and so has been subjected to a tensile force, whereas the bottom surface has been shortened by a compressive force.

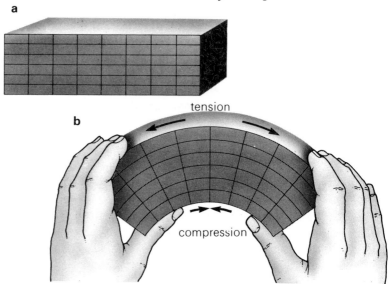

Figure 4.8

C Plastic deformation

Plastic deformation is *permanent irreversible deformation*. It is what happens when you squeeze a piece of modelling clay or warm bees-wax; they do not return to their original shape when you release the force on them.

Plastic deformation occurs in addition to elastic deformation; *all* solids deform elastically to some extent, *some* deform plastically as well. You can demonstrate this for yourself with articles such as a metal hair-grip or a polythene bag. If you release it after pulling it slightly, it will return to its original shape; this is elastic deformation. Increase the pull and you will find that beyond a certain point you start to deform the article permanently; this is plastic deformation. When you do this notice that, when you are pulling hard enough to produce plastic deformation, and then let it go, the bag or grip relaxes a little; part of the deformation is still elastic (reversible). The ability of a material to be deformed plastically is very important. It is one of the reasons why metals are so useful, for example, car bodies can be pressed to shape rather than being machined from a solid block of steel, a plumber can bend a copper pipe but could not do the same thing with a ceramic pipe, and so on.

More generally, a material that can undergo plastic deformation is usually more difficult to break: drop a glass mug and it will break, drop a metal mug and the worst thing that can happen is that it is dented. Glass is said to be *brittle* and a metal *tough*. In the next section we explore the meaning of each of these terms.

D Brittleness and toughness

If all the pieces of a broken pottery plate or glass window are recovered, they will often fit back together to form the original shape*. This is a common characteristic of **brittle** materials; they **brittleness** show virtually no plastic (permanent) deformation before breaking. Stone, ceramics and cast-iron are other examples of brittle materials, as are thermosetting adhesives, coatings and consolidants. They have a useful advantage in conservation work, especially if they are also weak, because they are more readily removed (mechanically) from an object.

Brittle materials are particularly susceptible to fracture under tensile stresses, but are generally stronger in compression. This can be useful. If you want to break a sheet of glass in a particular shape the technique is to scratch a line on the surface and "bend" the glass as shown in Figure 4.9. It should break neatly along the scratch. When a sheet of glass is bent like this, its top surface is stretched, in tension, and the bottom surface is shortened, in compression. The technique does not work if the scratch is on the compression surface.

The scratch in the surface is the key to understanding what happens. The tensile stress across the top surface of the sheet is the same at all points except near the scratch, which is the cause of a

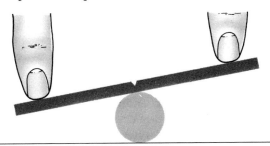

Figure 4.9

*Occasionally a pot may not fit back together perfectly because of strain produced by "internal stresses". The pot is then said to be "sprung". There is more about internal stress in Section 4E.

stress concentration

much higher local stress at its tip. Such high local stresses are called **stress concentrations** and they occur at notches, scratches, cracks and holes in materials that are otherwise subject to uniform stress. (Sharp bends or corners in an object can also be sources of stress concentration.) The sharper the defect, the greater is the stress concentration. Even if a material looks smooth, there will be minute surface defects that can act as sources of stress concentration, those on the surface of the shard shown in Figure 1.1 for instance. The tensile stresses acting in a material are, in effect, magnified around the source of a stress concentration.

As Figure 4.10(a) illustrates, a tensile stress tends to open up a crack and cause it to grow further into the material. A compressive stress acts to close the crack and inhibits its growth effectively (see Figure 4.10(b)).

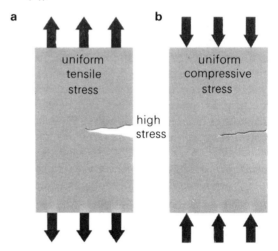

Figure 4.10

toughness

The ability of materials such as metals and thermoplastics above their glass transition temperature (see Chapter 3) to deform plastically makes them **tough**, which means that they are relatively difficult to break. A polythene bag may look flimsy but you would find it difficult to break one.

Plastic deformation makes a material tough because it can occur at the tip of a crack or tear and has a blunting effect, thereby reducing the stress concentration at the tip.

Some materials which do not exhibit plastic deformation can be tough because they possess another intrinsic crack-stopping mechanism. Wood and leather are examples. If you break a piece of wood you can fit the broken bits back together to form the original shape. They are brittle (that is, they do not exhibit plastic deformation), yet they are difficult to break. This apparent anomaly lies in the internal structure of these and similar materials. Figure 4.11 shows the fibrous cell structure of wood, which on a larger scale you see as the grain of the wood. The structural component of the cells – cellulose molecules – are aligned along the length of the fibres.

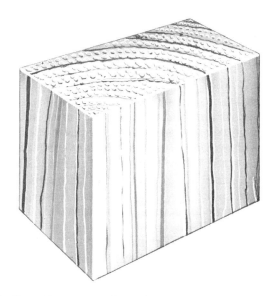

Figure 4.11 *The cell structure of wood.*

Cracks that attempt to grow across the grain in wood are simple diverted along the grain. Figure 4.12 illustrates this for a piece of wood loaded *along* the grain. Using this explanation, how would you

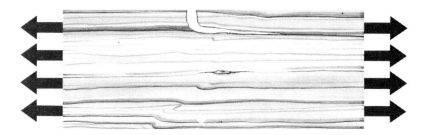

Figure 4.12 *Transverse cracks (across the grain) in a piece of wood are diverted along the grain.*

expect wood to behave when loaded across the grain? It should be weak and break easily, and, in fact, as you can see from Figure 4.3 the tensile strength of wood is about twenty times greater *along* the grain than *across* the grain. Most plants and other natural materials, including bone, horn and ivory are fibrous and therefore tough. Of course Nature ensures that the fibres are aligned in the direction of the largest stresses, and it pays when using these materials (or imitat-

fibre glass   ing them) to copy Nature. The material commonly known as **fibre-glass** or GRP (*glass-reinforced plastic*) is toughened by crack-stopping mechanisms similar in principle to those in wood. It has found a wide variety of structural uses, from the bodies of cars to replicas of museum objects. In this material the crack-stopping mechanism is provided by the interfaces between the glass fibres that are used to re-inforce the (polyester) thermosetting plastic.

This idea of making a material more difficult to break by incorporating fibres was appreciated many centuries before the effect could be accounted for. The ancient Egyptians made mud bricks incorporating straw, and in medieval Europe the plaster for surfacing the indoor walls of houses was re-inforced with horse-hair. In Victorian times, perfectly serviceable chairs were made from papier-mâché (pulped paper mixed with a starch-based binder); the cellulose fibres in the paper were the strengthening and toughening agents.

In the last three sections a number of concepts have been introduced and terms used in the description and explanation of how materials respond to mechanical forces. Check that you have understood them by tackling the following exercises. In the next section these ideas are used to examine briefly the general characteristics of adhesives and the joints made with them.

Exercise 4.1

Assume that the (peculiarly) shaped rod in Figure 4.13 is being pulled under a certain tensile force. On which cross-section, *A*, *B* or *C*, will the stress be greatest?

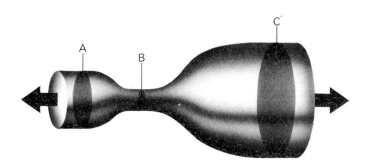

Figure 4.13

Exercise 4.2

The rods in Figure 4.14(a–c) are of different materials, and have been stretched by different amounts under the same tensile force; all had the same original length.

a In which rod has the greatest strain been produced?

b If the cross-sectional area of (c) is twice that of (a), which material has the higher Young's modulus?

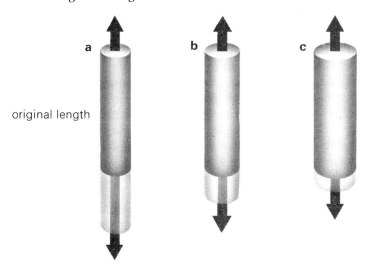

Figure 4.14

E Adhesives, adhesive joints and their mechanical behaviour

In earlier sections the way that an adhesive joint responds to a load has simply been referred to as the "strength" of a joint. You can now appreciate that a number of different material characteristics play a role in determining how well a joint responds to loads. You have been introduced to the formal language needed to consider these characteristics, in particular to definitions of force, stress, strain, ultimate tensile strength, Young's modulus, tough, brittle, elastic and plastic. This section looks at adhesives and joints using what you have learnt about these terms.

First, a general point that applies to the use of adhesives in most conservation work. The requirement is for an adhesive that will produce a joint that is strong enough to withstand the stresses to which the object is normally exposed. In the event of a failure, it is preferable for the *joint* to break either within the adhesive itself or at an interface between the adhesive and the adherend. In other words, the joint should not be so strong that the break occurs within the body of the object. In addition, there is the conflict between the need for the adhesive bonding to be strong enough to do its job and to last, yet weak enough to be broken should there be a need to take the joint apart. Consider some of the factors that influence the effectiveness of an adhesive joint – after all, whatever the required strength of the joint, along with its other characteristics, the ultimate aim is for it to be *predictable*.

The loads to which an object is subjected: those generated when it is handled or used, or accidentally knocked, or the weight of the parts, elicit a variety of responses in a joint through the stresses they generate.

It is the *stress* generated in a material (stress = force/area) that produces fracture. So, in general, for a given *load* on a joint, the lower the *stress*, the less likely the joint is to cause problems. This argument leads to two significant conclusions.

First, the greater the area of contact between the pieces to be joined, the lower is the stress generated in the joint by a given load; the load is spread over a greater area. This re-inforces the point made in Chapter 2, Section B that the adhesive should cover the whole of the available surface. It also emphasises that a joint with a large cross-sectional area will be stronger than one with a smaller area. This applies *if all other things are equal*, which brings us to the second conclusion.

For a given load, the stress is magnified in the vicinity of any source of *stress concentration*. Stress concentrations occur in any region where there is a change of cross-section or a flaw of some kind. Consider some examples. Fortunately, many of the joints needed in the repair of broken objects simply involve butt-jointing two pieces of the same cross-sectional area. This is essentially what happens when you stick together the pieces of a pot or plate, pieces of flat glass or regularly shaped pieces of metal. These are all examples of butt-jointing, which is illustrated in its most basic form in Figure 4.15(a).

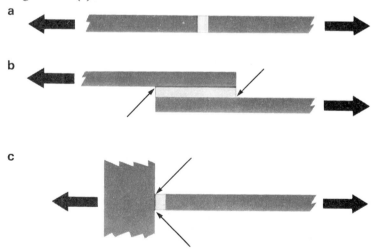

Figure 4.15 *Thin arrows mark the points where stress concentrations occur.*

Problems with stress concentrations arise with joints of the type shown in Figure 4.15(b) and (c). Examples of the type of joint shown in Figure 4.15(b) may not be common, but those of the type shown in Figure 4.15(c) are, joining of handles to pots and vases for instance.

Some idea of the origin of a stress concentration can be gained by considering a simple model of what happens on an atomic scale at the tip of a crack. The vertical rows of atoms depicted in Figure 4.16 can be visualised as a simple chain of atoms under tension due to an externally applied load. In this idealised crystal each chain is uniformly stressed.

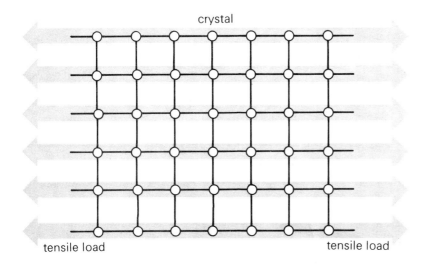

Figure 4.16a *The solid lines indicate idealised atomic bonds in a crystal. The shaded lines show the lines of stress through some of these bonds.*

Now, what happens if there is a crack in the structure?

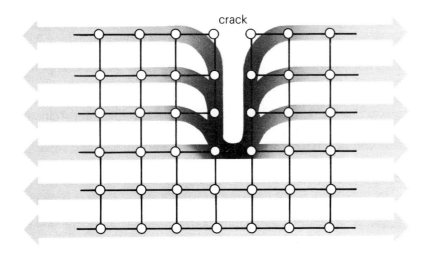

Figure 4.16b *The darker shading at the tip of the crack indicates an increase in stress.*

In effect, the crack is created by breaking some neighbouring bonds. This means that some of the chains of atoms are broken and, if the crystal is to remain whole, the load in these chains has to be taken by those that go round the end of the crack. The load in the broken chains is then concentrated on the one, or the few, atomic bonds at the tip of the crack. Clearly these bonds will break before their neighbours.

Figure 4.17 *The pattern of shear stress concentrations produced in a sample of clear resin containing a notch. Each dark line is a stress contour shown up by polarised light.*

A stress concentration forms at the tip of a scratch, crack or notch. This is why a textile material will tear easily once a small slit is cut in the edge and why glass breaks along the line scratched on its surface by the glazier. It is also the reason why shrinking of adhesive is undesirable. As the glue line recedes from the surface, a depression, and thus a stress concentration is formed.

Cracks will appear and propagate in the areas of highest stress, but it may not be clear why the stress is locally very high at a change in cross-section such as that shown in Figure 4.18(a).

Since the cross-sectional area of the thinner part is smaller, the stress in this part will be higher. In the bulk of the solid lines of stress will increase uniformly (see Figure 4.18(b)) and at either end the stress will be even across the material. However, near the surface several lines of stress converge and there is a concentration of stress in the atomic bonds at the point where the cross-section changes.

The number of stress lines that converge at this point is to some extent dependent on the degree of change in cross-section. If at each successive plane of atoms there is only a minute change in cross-section, the stress will increase uniformly without forming local concentrations (Figure 4.19.).

The example of handles is a good illustration of how, in the past, potters appreciated the problem and tried to overcome it, without

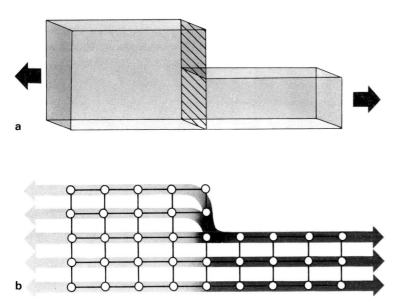

Figure 4.18 *Changes in stress and stress concentration at a change of cross-section. Darkness of shading indicates increased stress.*

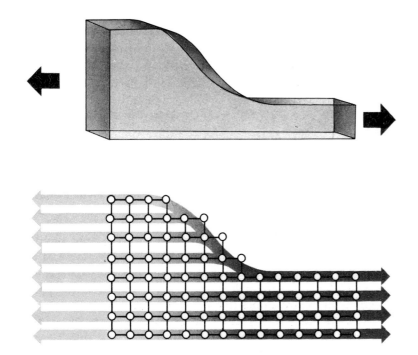

Figure 4.19 *A gradual increase in stress concentrations due to the gradual decrease in cross-section.*

a physical explanation of what goes on. Look at the handles on cups, vases, or jugs, and you will see that the join between the handle and the body of the object is smoothly curved: the greater the area of the section the lower is the stress, and the larger the radius of curvature (Figure 4.20) the lower is the stress concentration. If the change of section at the join is abrupt, as in Figure 4.15(c) the object is fragile.

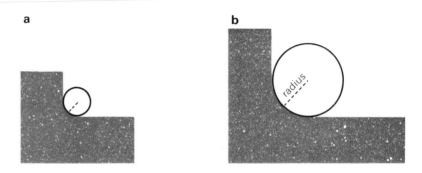

Figure 4.20 a *Small and* **b** *large radius of curvature.*

The important point here is that it is primarily the stress concentrations that determine how a joint behaves under load, and the larger the radius of curvature the smaller is the effect of the stress concentration. In a "lap-joint" (Figure 4.15(b)), the stress concentration at the arrowed points dominate how the joint responds to a load. The distance over which the pieces overlap is largely irrelevant compared with the width of the joint (its depth perpendicular to the page).

Incidentally, the lap-joint configuration illustrated in Figure 4.15(b) is the basis of *the peel or stripping strength test* that is often used to measure the effectiveness of a flexible coating on a rigid surface, for use as paint films for instance. This kind of test has also been used for assessing relining adhesives for painting conservation.

In Figure 4.21, the grey surface is a rigid and the unshaded surface is a flexible (low elastic modulus) material coated with the adhesive to be tested. When forces are applied as illustrated in Figure 4.21(a), the adhesive is subjected to shearing (sliding) forces. If the flexible material is pulled at an angle to the rigid surface, see Figure 4.21(b), the adhesive is exposed to both shearing (sliding) and tensile (pulling) forces in the presence of a stress concentration at the point indicated with a dark arrow.

As the angle of peel is increased the shear force decreases and the tensile force increases. In Figure 4.21(c) the adhesive is subjected to tensile forces only, but in the presence of a stress concentration. This **peel test** is the configuration used in a **peel test**.

peel strength The result of such a test is a value of the **peel strength** (measured as a *force* not a *stress*) and it depends on, for instance, the elastic

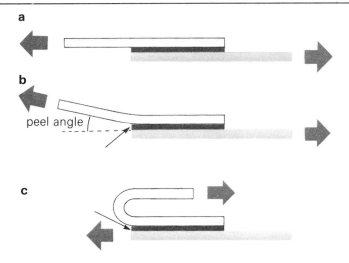

Figure 4.21 *The peel or stripping strength test.*

modulus of the rigid surface and the flexible material and the *peel angle*. Interpretation of this measure is complex and since peel strength is measured as a force (not stress), it can only be useful as a *comparative* test, that is, in measuring the behaviour of different adhesives using test pieces of exactly the same size and shape and in exactly the same geometrical configuration. Obviously these tests have to be standardised or different people's results could not be compared.

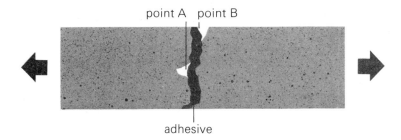

Figure 4.22 *Possible sites for stress concentrations, caused by inadequate preparation of a joint.*

On a smaller scale, flaws in a joint, such as bubbles in the solid adhesive or cracks in the adhesive or at the interfaces of the joint, are major stress concentrations; any source of a crack is a source of trouble. Figure 4.22 shows, schematically, two examples of this, at points *A* and *B*, in a butt-joint. Both of these could occur from inadequate preparation of the joint, particularly if the surfaces of the object are not covered completely with adhesive and/or not pressed together firmly. Type *B* could also arise from a flake of material from the broken object which is only loosely attached to the break surface. Under the tensile load shown in Figure 4.22 both flaws would tend to grow as cracks because the force acts to open them up.

Having dealt with some of the factors that affect the *strength* of a joint, what about its stiffness requirements? Ideally, the elastic modulus (or simply elasticity) of the solid adhesive should be the same as that of the object material. In some cases, this is an obvious requirement – for instance, joining pieces of a stiff object with a flexible glue might produce undesirable distortion of the object.

There is another, less obvious, reason. If part of an object has a different stiffness (elastic modulus) from other parts, any stresses that arise are not evenly distributed through the object; the stress may be concentrated in particular regions. To illustrate this point, consider the veneered piece of wood in Figure 4.23:

Figure 4.23

Suppose that it is subjected to a tensile load that stretches it by a certain amount, as shown. Young's modulus = stress/strain, and since the strain produced in the adhesive and the veneer is the same, if the Young's modulus of the veneer is the greater, so then will be the stress produced in it. Correspondingly, if the adhesive has the greater Young's modulus, a greater stress will be generated within it. In either case the shear stress created is acting to break the adhesive bonds at the interfaces between the adhesive and the bonded surfaces. In conservation work, a stiffer adhesive is preferred because it usually means that, if failure occurs the adhesive breaks rather than the object.

Before concluding this section on the mechanical behaviour of adhesives and adhesive joints, one further point about stress and strength should be introduced. This is that stresses can be generated within the body of an object in the absence of an externally applied load. These **internal stresses** as they are called can exceed the strength of the material and therefore lead to fracture. Any process that leads to part of an object undergoing elastic deformation relative to those parts to which it is attached will set up internal stresses. An important example of such a process in adhesive joints is **thermal expansion**. Most materials expand when they are heated, and some more than others. Thermal expansion is similar to stiffness in that its value depends on the magnitude and character of the bonding forces between the atoms or molecules in a material. The stronger the bonding, the smaller is the thermal expansion – the smaller the distance the atoms and molecules move apart. For example, polymers bonded by secondary forces expand more than materials, such as metals and ceramics, that are held together by primary bonds. Thus, for a given rise in temperature, many adhesives will expand more

internal stress

thermal expansion

than materials they are joining. When this happens it is equivalent to a greater strain occurring in the adhesive than in the adherend, with the result that internal stresses are created.

This effect can be of practical significance in a number of ways. Imagine coating a thin strip of material with molten beeswax, or some other melt-freeze adhesive as illustrated in Figure 4.24. When the adhesive cools, solidifies, and continues to cool down, it contracts progressively. (In other words it gets shorter.) Provided that the beeswax remains stuck to the thin strip, the strip is forced to bend to the shape illustrated in Figure 4.24(b); the beeswax is under compression and the strip under tension.

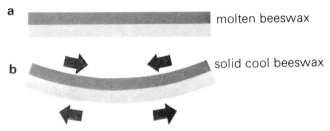

Figure 4.24 *A molten beeswax layer on a thin strip setting and causing the strip to warp as the wax contracts on cooling.*

Of course, the bending occurs in this example because the strip is unconstrained. If the strip were a bulky object, or, say, held at its ends, the internal stresses would still be there. Similar effects are produced by solvent adhesives. In these cases the contraction is not due to cooling but to the shrinkage associated with the evaporation of the solvent.

Figure 4.25 *Distortion of a plywood frame due to a coating of **a** animal glue. **b** soluble nylon. **c** a poly(vinyl acetate) emulsion.*

Related effects arise if a solid adhesive expands by absorbing moisture. You can see that the behaviour of an adhesive is complex, and that the problems of, say, solvent evaporation or water absorption can affect the stability of an adhesive joint. This is the subject of the next chapter.

5

How long will it last?

A Physical changes
A1 Diffusion
A2 Polymer solvents and solubility
B Chemical change
C Further thoughts on the degradation
   of adhesive joints
D Accelerated ageing tests

How long will it last?

How long an adhesive joint lasts obviously depends on what degradation processes are taking place and how fast. Physical or chemical changes occur in the adhesive or adherend that make the joint incapable of coping with the mechanical loads acting on it or with the internal stresses that are often generated by those changes. Paradoxically, perhaps, many of the processes that lead to degradation may be harnessed by you when you wish to remove an adhesive joint from an object. Consequently, exploring these processes, in this chapter, has a double purpose.

Clearly, except for circumstances in which an adhesive joint is subjected to an abnormally high load (when it is dropped for instance), it should be permanent, provided that it is chemically stable and in a controlled harmless environment. However, neither of these conditions are found in practice.

The chemical elements that make up a metal or alloy are not in a stable state compared with their natural state as minerals in the Earth; and they react with chemical compounds in the atmosphere, such as oxygen, sulphur dioxide, hydrogen sulphide, carbon dioxide, and water. This is why, for instance, rust forms on many iron alloys, and silver becomes tarnished. Similarly, both synthetic organic polymers and materials made from natural organic polymers (such as paper and leather) oxidise in air, leading to discoloration and embrittlement. The presence of water can have quite different effects on polymeric adhesives; it can be absorbed and produce swelling, and hence internal stresses (in, for instance, adhesives based on nylon), and it can react chemically with the polymer to produce both structural weakening and undesirable products (such as acetic acid from cellulose acetate and polyvinyl acetate). Finally, embrittlement can be produced in an adhesive that loses a component by slow evaporation. This applies particularly to solvent adhesives which retain some of the solvent and to adhesives that have constituents added, such as plasticisers.

In this chapter the main physical changes that can lead to degradation are explored. Chemical changes are dealt with next and, finally, the degradation of joints in practice. The distinction between chemical and physical changes was made in Book 1. Chemical changes are processes in which the primary bonds between atoms are re-organised to produce new chemical compounds.

A Physical changes

Physical changes usually involve a change of volume due to the gain or loss of material, or the rearrangement of the existing atoms or molecules. The extent and rate of volume change depend primarily on two phenomena: *diffusion* and *solubility*.

A1 Diffusion

You know from earlier books in this series that the atoms and molecules in a solid are never entirely static. Even at very low temperatures atoms vibrate and the bonds in molecules stretch and contract. In fact, atoms and molecules are sometimes able to move through the bulk of a solid; small molecules are more mobile than large ones as they can squeeze through the gaps between other **diffusion**   molecules. This movement is called **diffusion** and it plays an important, often crucial, role in many processes. For instance, it determines the rate at which a solvent is removed from a joint when a solvent adhesive is used. The small solvent molecules have to diffuse through the tangle of much larger and less mobile polymer molecules. As a reaction-type adhesive sets, the monomers have to pass through the rapidly forming polymer network to reach the appropriate reaction site and so the rate of diffusion may determine the rate of setting. One of the main reasons for applying a coating to an object is to protect it by providing a barrier between the object and harmful chemicals. Clearly, in such cases, the most effective coatings are those which minimise diffusion through them of the harmful species; more will be said about this in Chapter 7.

This section firstly deals with how diffusion occurs in a crystalline solid composed of atoms bound together by primary bonds, such as a metal or a ceramic and then moves on to discuss diffusion in polymers, which has some rather different characteristics but which can be understood in terms of the scientific models introduced here and earlier.

Diffusion in inorganic crystals
The atoms in a crystal form a regular arrangement as a result of a balance in the chemical bonds acting between them. As you know from Book 2, atoms are in a constant state of motion which determines

the kinetic energy they possess. The higher the temperature, the greater their kinetic energy, and it is this kinetic energy that drives the process of diffusion. However, it does not drive atoms in any particular direction: diffusion is, in fact, the result of the haphazard wanderings of many individual atoms.

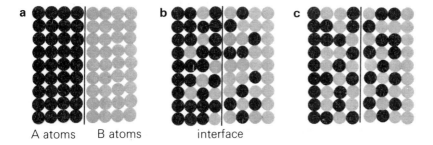

A atoms   B atoms   interface

Figure 5.1 *Diffusion between two different metals.*
Type A atoms are indicated as dark and type B as light.

Figure 5.1 shows various stages in the diffusion that occurs when two different metals are placed in intimate contact. This is similar to what we saw happening in the soldering process in Chapter 3. In this very simplified example just a very small part of a plane that cuts through the pair of metals will be considered. If the metals are elements of type *A* and type *B* (shown as dark and light respectively in Figure 5.1) then at first all the atoms at one side of the interface will be *A* atoms and all those on the other side will be *B* atoms. We must assume that an atom of *A* will be as stable when completely surrounded by atoms of *B* as it is surrounded by atoms of *A*, and that a *B* atom is equally stable with either *A* or *B* atoms as nearest neighbours. That is, we assume that the metals *A* and *B* are completely soluble in one another, as, for instance, copper and nickel are.

Now consider an *A* atom in Figure 5.1(a) at the interface between the two metals. It can "jump" in any one of six directions – up, down, to the left, to the right, into the page, and out from the page. (In this model a "jump" refers to an exchange with a neighbouring atom.) The only one of these possibilities that makes a difference to the overall distribution of atoms is a jump to the right and so of all the jumps made by all of the atoms, only a fraction lead to an obvious change. In Figure 5.1(b) a few atoms of *A* and *B* have diffused across the interface, and the distribution of *A* and *B* atoms is being smoothed out.

As diffusion continues, the distribution of *A* and *B* atoms will be progressively evened out until the distribution represented by Figure 5.1(c) is reached. Here the interface has actually disappeared

— the solid on one side is indistinguishable from that on the other. Although diffusion will still continue, it will make no difference to the overall distribution of the atoms. Statistically, for every *A* atom jumping to the right, say, there is one jumping to the left.

The grossly simplified model of diffusion described here has the sole purpose of showing how the random migration of atoms produces a change in composition. It ignores a number of factors that are important in real materials, and, in particular, it assumes that diffusion of *A* atoms in the metal *B* is as easy, or as difficult, as that of *B* atoms in the metal *A*. Since the magnitude of the chemical bonding between *A* atoms, between *B* atoms, and between *A* and *B* atoms, will all be different, the relative ease of diffusion of the two species will be different.

composition gradient

It has been found by experiment that the rate of diffusion is proportional to the **composition gradient**. Composition gradient describes the way composition changes with distance. In Figure 5.1(a) the gradient is very great across the interface as there is a total change in composition from all *A* to all *B* in a very small distance. The gradient is levelling out in Figure 5.1(b) as the distance between mostly *A* and mostly *B* increases. The composition gradient in Figure 5.1(c) is zero as there is uniform composition throughout the solid.

rate of diffusion

The **rate of diffusion** can be thought of in terms of the *net* number of atoms that migrate across a given plane within the solid (such as the interface in Figure 5.1) in a given time. This number can be represented by the letter *J*.

The proportional relationship between the rate of diffusion *J* and composition gradient, *C*, can be expressed as a very simple equation:

$$J = DC$$

diffusion coefficient
diffusivity

This means that the rate *J* is equal to some number, *D*, multiplied by *C*, the composition gradient. *D* is called the **diffusion coefficient** (or **diffusivity**). It is constant for one material diffusing through another material at a particular temperature. The units still most commonly used are cm^2/sec or $cm^2/hour$ even though these are not the recommended SI units.

Fick's Law

The relationship described above is called **Fick's Law** but it is not the name or the symbols that are important, it is the simple relationship between rate and concentration (composition is the concentration of one substance, *A*, in another, *B*). Values for the diffusion coefficient can be determined experimentally, for instance, by surrounding a material with a radioactive isotope of the required chemical element and monitoring the progress of the isotope through the material. Figure 5.2 gives you an idea of the sort of values obtained for different materials under different conditions; they are very approximate and only give an idea of the ranges found in practice.

You will notice that there is an incredibly large difference between the values. Unfortunately the diffusion coefficient does not give a direct measure of the distance over which diffusion occurs. However, since diffusion is the overall result of the *random walk* of individual atoms, the random walk can be analysed to give the

Material and diffusion species	D = Diffusion coefficient cm^2/sec (very approximate)	Time for average atom or molecule to diffuse 1 mm.
single atoms in metal (25°C)	10^{-25}	10^{23} secs (never!)
single atoms in metal (near melting point)	10^{-8}	10^{6} secs (about 12 days)
single atoms in a liquid metal	10^{-4}	10^{2} secs (about 2 minutes)
small molecules (for example, O_2) in polymers	10^{9}	10^{-22} secs (immediately!)

Figure 5.2

average behaviour of an atom. In a certain time, call it t, an average atom migrates a distance which can be calculated as $\sqrt{Dt}$ from its starting point ($\sqrt{Dt}$ is the square root* of what you get by multiplying D by t). So, the distance $\sqrt{Dt}$ is that over which the composition can change substantially in a time, t, due to diffusion. To give you an idea of what this means, Figure 5.2 includes the time it takes, on average, for each of the diffusing species to travel 1 mm. The range is enormous. A detailed explanation of why the difference between the diffusion of atoms in metals at ordinary temperatures and of small molecules in polymers is so great is complex and beyond the scope of this book. However, qualitatively, the reasons are not difficult to see.

Consider first the difference between a solid and a liquid metal. In a solid metal the atoms are strongly bound together by primary bonds and packed tightly together in a crystalline array; the arrangement is illustrated schematically in Figure 5.3(a). In the liquid, the atoms are more loosely packed, see Figure 5.3(b), in which the increased distance between the atoms has been greatly exaggerated.

a  b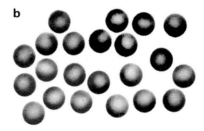

Figure 5.3

More energy is required by an atom in order to move into a neighbouring site in a crystal than in the liquid, mainly because it has to disturb its neighbouring atoms much more. The (relatively) very fast rates of diffusion that can occur in metal crystals near their melting point simply illustrates the dramatic effect of the greater thermal energy available at higher temperatures in aiding a diffusing atom to overcome its bonding forces.

The square root of a number, for example 9, is the number, in this case 3, which multiplied by itself gives the original number, 9. Thus, $3 \times 3 = 9$, that is, $\sqrt{9} = 3$.

Diffusion in polymeric materials

Diffusion of the molecules in a thermoplastic material differs from that of atoms in a crystal in two important ways. Firstly, the polymer molecules are very large and have a complex structure, and so very little movement past other molecules occurs. Secondly, since the use of such materials is usually limited to temperatures below about 100°C, the available thermal energy is much less than that for metals at higher temperatures. Consequently, diffusion of the polymeric molecules in a thermoplastic below its glass transition temperature (see Chapter 2, Section D2), can be assumed to be negligible. Of course, in thermosetting plastics the rigid network polymer molecule will not undergo diffusion either. However, smaller molecules can diffuse within and through a polymeric material and often very readily. This is because of the relative openness of the molecular structure – particularly in amorphous polymers – and because, in thermoplastics, the molecules are only held together by weak secondary forces.

In a thermoset the polymeric network is relatively open and diffusion will be easy, depending on the size of the diffusing molecule and the size of the spaces in the network. Clearly, the more frequently cross-links occur along the polymer molecule, the smaller are the gaps in the network, and consequently the smaller are the molecules that can readily diffuse through the structure. Similarly, amorphous thermoplastics permit more rapid diffusion than do crystalline polymers. Diffusion through an amorphous thermoplastic varies sharply, depending on whether the temperature is above or below the glass transition temperature, T_g. When the temperature is above T_g, the mobility of the polymer chains allows paths to open up for the diffusing molecules; at temperatures below T_g, the structure is rigid and consequently diffusion is more difficult – it requires the aid of more thermal energy, that is higher temperatures.

Polymer	State	Relative permeability to oxygen at 30°C
Poly(ethylene terephthalate)	crystalline	1
Polystyrene (PS)	amorphous	50
Rubber	"rubbery"	1000

Figure 5.4

permeability

This is shown in Figure 5.4, where polymers in different states are shown to have very different rates of permeability to oxygen molecules. **Permeability** is a complex phenomenon involving diffusion and solubility factors. A small polar molecule will permeate a polymer with polar side-groups more readily than a non-polar molecule. Not only can the polar molecule pass through gaps in the network because of its small size, it can do so because it is compatible with (effectively soluble in) the polymer: *like dissolves like* (see Book 2, Chapter 3) can be extended to *like permeates like'*. This is demonstrated by the data in Figure 5.5 which shows the relative permeability to water vapour.

Polymer	Relative permeability to H$_2$O at 90% relative humidity and 25°C
Poly(vinylidene chloride) (PVDC)	1
Polythene (PE)	10
Polyester (for example Melinex) (PET)	100
Cellulose acetate (CA)	5000

Figure 5.5

Poly (vinylidene) chloride is built up from CH$_2$=CCl$_2$ monomer units and as a co-polymer with vinyl chloride is the basis of water-proof films such as Saran. Polythene has no polar groups on its hydrocarbon chains whereas polyesters have carbonyl groups at regular intervals in their structure. Cellulose acetate, formed by treating cellulose with acetic anhydride ((CH$_3$CO)$_2$O) has the polar acetate group and some remaining —OH groups which are compatible with the water molecules.

An obvious consequence of diffusion is the *swelling* that occurs when molecules migrate into and occupy the gaps in a polymeric structure, particularly in thermosets and amorphous thermoplastics. Before developing this point further, it will be useful to explore briefly polymer solvents and solubility.

A2 Polymer solvents and solubility

Solvents, solutes and the factors that influence the solubility of one chemical compound in another were discussed in some detail in Chapter 3 of Book 2. You would find it useful to remind yourself of the main arguments described in that chapter before proceeding with this section.

The **solubility of polymers** is of particular significance in con-   **polymer solubility**
servation work. Firstly, many adhesives, coatings and consolidants that are used need to be in solution in order for them to be applied effectively. Secondly, dissolution is an important means of removing old joints that are no longer required.

When a long-chain (thermoplastic) polymeric material dissolves in a solvent, the primary bonds holding the atoms together in each molecule remain intact; each polymer molecule retains its identity. This is demonstrated by the fact that the polymer molecules can be recovered from a solution by, say, evaporation – rather as salt can be recovered from brine. To form a polymer solution molecules of the solvent penetrate the polymeric structure and separate the polymer molecules from one another. This is depicted in a simplified way in Figure 5.6 (overleaf).

For a polymeric material to form such a solution, the secondary bonds between adjacent polymer molecules must be broken. This is favoured when the bonds between the solvent molecules and the polymer molecules are equal to, or stronger than, those between

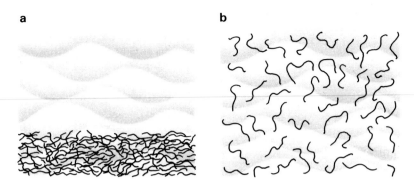

Figure 5.6 *Schematic representation of a polymer dissolving in a liquid.*

polymer molecules. One consequence of this as you saw in Chapter 3 of Book 2, is that solvent molecules with polar side-groups are likely to be able to penetrate and ultimately dissolve polymer molecules with polar side-groups. Thus polar liquids such as water, alcohols and ketones are widely used as solvents; cellulose nitrate dissolves in ketones or esters, for instance, and poly(vinyl alcohol) (PVAL) is soluble in water.

Many thermoplastics have limited solubility in solvents in the sense that only small amounts of solvent molecules enter and permeate the polymer material. As discussed in Section D of Chapter 2 such solvents act as *plasticisers*; they increase the flow (plastic deformation) capability of the material, reduce its stiffness, and in effect reduce its glass transition temperature. The absorption of such molecules into the gaps between the polymer molecules usually causes the material to swell. As you would expect, because they have a more open structure, amorphous long-chain polymers permit more rapid diffusion than highly crystalline polymers. Since swelling requires diffusion of the relevant molecule, materials of high crystallinity have a more limited tendency to swell.

If an established adhesive joint, coating or consolidant absorbs solvent molecules, and water is the obvious and most important **swelling** example, the processes of *plasticisation* and **swelling** can lead to degradation. This is looked at in Section C. (Remember that the same processes can also be the means by which old restoration materials are removed from an object.)

Cross-linked (thermosetting) polymers cannot be dissolved in the sense described here. Since they consist of a network in which the atoms are held together by primary bonds, individual polymer chains cannot be separated by solvent molecules. However, chemically compatible liquids may penetrate them to some extent and produce swelling which may eventually soften or crack the material. Again, this can lead to degradation, and also be a means of removing old materials from an object.

B Chemical change

A chemical change, as stated at the beginning of this chapter, involves a chemical reaction (see Book 1, Chapter 2), that is a process in which the primary bonds between atoms are re-arranged to produce new chemical compounds. Generally speaking, the parent molecules in the natural and synthetic polymeric materials used in conservation work are relatively stable chemically. However, there is one particularly important exception to this statement: their susceptibility to oxidation (the subject of oxidation was introduced in Chapter 7 of Book 2). Although particular polymers are prone to attack by specific chemicals other than oxygen, for example polystyrene reacts with sulphuric acid, polythene with chlorine, such materials are either not normally used in conservation work or the troublesome chemical is not present.

Consider oxidation. It should not be surprising that most organic polymers suffer from oxidation; after all they are usually flammable (combustion being rapid oxidation). This is one reason why very few organic plastics used in engineering are useful above about 100°C. However, for most applications at ordinary temperatures the rate of oxidation is tolerably slow or it can be controlled, but, unfortunately, in conservation work the required time scales are relatively long. In adhesives, coatings and consolidants, oxidation can cause degradation and hence embrittlement or discoloration.

A useful illustration of the embrittlement produced by oxidation is provided by natural rubber and its synthetic counterparts (these are usually called **elastomers**). Oxygen atoms, like sulphur atoms, can form two covalent bonds, and can therefore provide similar cross-links to those made by sulphur in the vulcanisation of rubber, see Figure 2.9. This is what happens as an ageing process in the rubber used in, for example, car tyres. Progressively, oxygen atoms form more cross-links, and, as you know from Section C in Chapter 2, the greater the number of cross-links the harder and more rigid is the material. In effect, the rubber becomes more like a thermosetting plastic and, in a car tyre, the rubber is unable to undergo the large elastic deformation required every time the wheel revolves. As a result the rubber begins to crack at the surface; you can often see such cracks ("perishing") on the walls of old tyres.

In a similar way, when other polymeric materials are embrittled by oxidation it is usually due to the creation of cross-links (the other main reason for embrittlement is due to the loss of plasticiser or solvent by evaporation, see Chapter 5, Section C). After a great deal of research work it is becoming clear that oxidation does not normally occur by direct reaction between oxygen and a polymer chain. It is thought that under normal temperatures and conditions certain highly reactive impurities incorporated in the material during its synthesis or processing are normally involved. The end product is that a C—C or C—H bond is attacked. Details of the mechanisms are beyond the level of this text, but from this simple description it

elastomers

is clear that polymeric materials used in conservation should be as pure as possible. Another reason for this is that discoloration is often due to the oxidation of impurities, as in phenol formaldehyde for instance which is always yellow or brown.

photo-oxidation

In some polymeric material oxidation is accelerated by ultra-violet light. This is called **photo-oxidation**. Again the mechanisms are complex and diverse but it seems that the breaking of C—C or C—H bonds does not usually occur; the C===O bond appears to be much more susceptible, which means that polyesters, polyurethanes and polyamides (such as nylon) are particularly prone to photo-oxidation. Note, however, acrylics are generally much more stable, so the whole picture is definitely not simple.

anti-oxidants

Oxidation can be inhibited, but not arrested completely, by incorporating **anti-oxidants** in the formulation of a plastic. These normally work by either reacting preferentially with oxygen that diffuses into the polymer or with the active impurities that may be present.

To summarise: in chemical terms the more stable polymeric materials are, the less they are likely to undergo chemical change. In other words, reactive molecular structures and components should be avoided. From this and earlier chapters in this text, you can start to recognise a number of points about the structure of polymers that could encourage chemical stability:

- Avoiding materials containing unsaturated polymer chains – those with a $C=C$ bond such as rubbers and unsaturated polyesters.

- Avoiding materials containing polymers with highly reactive side-groups such as C—Cl.

- (Unless objects are shielded from ultra-violet light) avoiding the use of polymeric materials containing $C=O$ bonds.

- Using materials that are as pure as possible.

These points are generally true but there are notable individual exceptions, such as some stable and very useful polyesters and acrylics.

C Further thoughts on the degradation of adhesive joints

Since the function of an adhesive joint is to hold pieces of an object together, that is, to resist loads attempting to pull the pieces apart, the joint will have failed when it can no longer withstand these loads. However, in conservation work the requirements are often more demanding. For instance, a joint may be judged unacceptable, although still structurally sound, because it has become distorted or discoloured. The main reasons for discoloration were discussed in the previous section, and so here only degradation processes that involve the mechanical behaviour of a joint, that is its responses to mechanical loads, will be considered.

Adhesives are applied in liquid form and end up as a solid in the completed joint – the reasons behind these requirements were examined in Chapter 1, (Section C). In a melt-freeze adhesive the liquid cools and freezes to a solid of the same composition. Solution adhesives and reaction adhesives are not so straightforward. To produce a solid joint, the solvent in the former case, and the water, or other products, of the polymerisation process in the latter, have to be removed. The molecules involved are usually small and most of them diffuse to the surface and evaporate during the time the adhesive is hardening. During this stage the adhesive is in a paste-like condition with a fairly open structure and so diffusion is easy. However, some of the solvent or polymerisation product will remain in the solid joint and diffuse out over a long period.

The important point about these changes from liquid to solid and the loss of solvent from the solid is that they are always accompanied by a shrinkage of the adhesive. This **shrinkage** is important not only because it can lead to distortion of the object – particularly if the joint does not have an even thickness – but also because it produces internal stresses. The consequences of this are explored with an idealised adhesive joint illustrated in Figure 5.7; to demonstrate the effects, the thickness and shrinkage of the adhesive have been exaggerated.

adhesive shrinkage

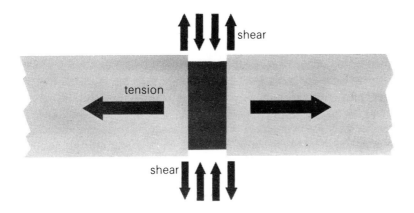

Figure 5.7

On shrinking, the molecules in the adhesive move closer together and therefore pull the pieces of the object being joined closer together. If the other ends of the pieces are fixed, as they would be in many cases, say replacing the handle on a pot, a piece in a broken plate and so on, contraction of the adhesive creates a pull (*tensile* force) on the joint or the pieces being joined. If these internal stresses reach values that exceed the strength of the adhesive, or the bonding at the interfaces, or of the pieces of the object, fracture will occur.

These stresses can be important, particularly for very fragile materials, such as old fabrics and paper, and in joints that have become weak as a result of chemical changes.

This is not the only effect. Shrinkage will occur in all directions within the adhesive which means that internal *shear* stresses are also created (see Figure 5.7). These stresses will act directly on the adhesive joint. The material on either side of the joint is deformed elastically in shear which means that the original chemical bonds across the interface will be distorted.

This is an important effect because regions of elastic strain are more prone to attack by chemicals in the environment than those that are not strained. Such attack could progressively remove the bonds at the interface between the adhesive and the adherend with consequent weakening of the joint. Under these conditions the interface could be, for example, the preferred site for oxidation or a preferred route for diffusion of solvent molecules such as water. The latter process of degradation has been found to be particularly important for adhesives used under normal weathering conditions. Epoxy resins are an example.

The "drying out" of an adhesive joint, with the consequent creation of internal stresses and an increased susceptibility to chemical attack, is one of the main factors that can ultimately lead to the complete breakdown of a joint. Clearly, the more an adhesive shrinks as it ages, the more likely it is to degrade and eventually break down. So, for instance, the amount of solvent used in a solvent adhesive should be kept to a minimum.

Another very important aspect of the loss of solvent during ageing is that in many adhesives (cellulose nitrate, poly(vinyl acetate) and some acrylics are examples) small amounts of residual solvent molecules act as a plasticiser. If the solvent-free adhesive is a weak brittle material, the progressive loss of solvent will lead to embrittlement. This is an inevitable process that will be made worse by **photo-degradation** chemical changes such as oxidation and **photo-degradation** (decay caused by light).

So far only the creation of internal stresses as a result of shrinkage has been looked at. Stresses can also be created by the reverse process, that is swelling (expansion). If objects on which the conservation treatments have involved joining, coating or consolidation are kept under the mild and relatively constant atmosphere of a museum or similar place, the problems associated with the absorption of liquids and consequent swelling are seldom significant. Although moisture from a normal atmosphere may diffuse into, say, a joint, it will be in insufficient amounts for the internal stresses produced by any swelling to be of consequence; as indicated earlier, the disruption of adhesive bonds by water molecules is likely to be much more important. Swelling, however, is a crucial problem in the restoration of waterlogged objects made from timber, paper and similar materials. The internal stresses produced by swelling on the one hand, and by the contraction produced in drying timber on the other, can readily lead to cracking, warping and failure. These effects are produced, for instance, when the relative humidity of the atmosphere fluctuates.

A further undesirable effect of the ageing of adhesives (as well as coatings and consolidants) is that some evolve damaging chemicals. These chemicals may be fumes that are toxic and/or damaging to other materials. For instance, cellulose acetate and poly(vinyl acetate) can release acetic acid, which accelerates the corrosion of lead; many of the solvents used in solvent adhesives are poisonous.

This discussion has stated fairly emphatically how difficult it is to choose a satisfactory adhesive. Selection is made more difficult by the fact that the technical requirements of commercially available adhesives are often less demanding than those of conservation, particularly with respect to discoloration. If you do consider commercial adhesives, try to use those that have been well-tried and characterised, and if experimenting with new ones it is best to use those that contain as little impurity as possible, stable anti-oxidants, and a minimum of solvent or plasticiser. An alternative is to carry out accelerated ageing tests on the adhesives you consider using.

D Accelerated ageing tests

One way of estimating the ageing characteristics of an adhesive is to carry out tests which accelerate the effects of time, one of which is to observe what happens at a higher temperature. Such tests are quite often used (and, when carefully controlled, they can give strong indications of the likely natural behaviour). Unfortunately, the approach is fraught with problems because a variety of factors determine the ageing behaviour of a joint and because by their very nature, the tests are artificial. As you will appreciate by now, the important processes of degradation involve either chemical reactions of some sort, or physical changes that depend on diffusion; usually there are a number going on simultaneously.

You know from Section A in this chapter that the rate of diffusion increases very rapidly with increasing temperature, and chemical reactions exhibit the same behaviour – this is why, for example, epoxy resins cure faster on a hot day than on a cold day. The rate of diffusion and rate of chemical reaction are controlled by the activation energies of the processes. As you learnt in Book 2, only a small number of molecules have sufficient energy to cause a chemical change on collision with another molecule. Similarly, only a small number of molecules will have sufficient energy to squeeze through a gap in a polymer network. As the temperature rises the proportion of sufficiently energetic molecules rises dramatically (exponentially, see Book 2, Chapter 7). The dramatic effect of this is tabulated in Figure 5.8 using two hypothetical chemical reactions that proceed *at the same rate at 20°C*, but have different activation energies.

Temperature °C	Rate of reaction *A* (number of times faster than at 20°C)	Rate of reaction *B* (number of times faster than at 20°C)
30	2	3
40	4	9
50	8	27
60	16	81
70	32	243
80	64	729

Figure 5.8

The rate of reaction *A* is assumed to increase by a factor of two for each 10°C rise in temperature, and that of reaction *B* by a factor of three. The Figure illustrates both the usefulness and the main disadvantage of accelerated ageing tests. First, such a test on a material in which, say, reaction *A* is occurring will, in principle, provide the result of about five years' ageing at 20°C in only a month at 80°C. Unfortunately, in most materials several different thermally-activated processes occur simultaneously at normal temperatures. Since they all have different activation energies an accelerated ageing test will exaggerate some reactions more than others. You can see from the data in Figure 5.8 that reaction *B*, which has the same rate as reaction *A* at 20°C, is proceeding more than eleven times faster at 80°C. If reaction *B* is the most important one in natural ageing, the test will be useful, but, if not, misleading results will be obtained. Clearly, the lower the temperature at which accelerated ageing tests are carried out, the more reliable the results will be because the difference between the rates of the different reactions will be lessened. On the other hand, the higher the temperature the shorter the time in which indications become clear. In practice, the conditions used are typically four weeks at 70°C.

Accelerated tests of discoloration or degradation in light which use very intense light for a short duration to simulate lower light levels over a longer period also have disadvantages.

Photo-oxidation of polymers is a stepwise series of reactions, some of which are slower than others. If a reaction occurs as a series of steps the rate of the overall reaction is determined by the slowest step (the "bottleneck"). Some of the stages in photo-oxidation are *activated by light* and some are *thermally activated*. Increasing the intensity of light may increase the rate of one step but this may not be the one that fully determines the rate of the complete reaction.

Bearing these reservations in mind, accelerated ageing tests can give useful pointers to those factors that are important in degradation. The tests are likely to be more effective if the adhesive is tested in conjunction with the material with which the joint is to be made, since diffusion of chemicals into the material may influence the degradation processes.

Testing some of the other characteristics of an adhesive is possible. In particular, the shrinkage of an adhesive can be examined by pouring it into a wooden frame so that an attached film is formed. The subsequent distortion can be easily observed. Equally, the chemical reactivity between a material and an adhesive can be tested by putting them in close proximity in, say, a test-tube. Such tests give indications about which adhesives and materials are chemically incompatible, but again these tests are at elevated temperatures.*

You will now see that a variety of tests can be devised for individual jobs; many of them are useful although it is important to bear in mind that they are unlikely to afford accurate predictions, only indications. Consequently it is unwise for a conservator to become too absorbed in carrying out detailed tests of this kind; their relevance is limited and their interpretation difficult.

*For further information on these and other tests, see Blackshaw and Daniels, **The Conservator**, vol. 2, 1979.*

6

Coatings

Coatings

An amazing number and variety of coatings are used on objects, and all sorts of terms are employed to describe them (paint, emulsion, varnish, lacquer, enamel, glaze). Nowadays, these terms are often used interchangeably and a brief general definition of each may help you to avoid possible confusion.

A **paint** is a suspension of solid pigment in a suitable liquid which when applied to a surface dries to form a solid film. An **emulsion paint** is one in which the solid (a mixture of polymer and pigment) is in the form of finely dispersed particles in suspension in a liquid, and **varnishes** and **lacquers** are simply unpigmented coatings. Varnishes and lacquers usually have a characteristic hard and glossy surface (although matt finishes are also possible). Originally, varnishes and lacquers were based on the sap from trees; varnish from the tung, or Chinese "varnish" tree, and lacquer from the Japanese "lacquer" tree – hence the terms Japan lacquer and japanning. Traditionally, **enamels** and **glazes** were vitrified (glass) coatings produced by a firing process, but the terms now cover any coating with a glass-like appearance and may include organic polymers.

paint

emulsion paint

varnish
lacquer

enamel, glaze

A The requirements of a good coating

This chapter is short because the requirements of a coating and the means by which it is produced have a very great deal in common with those for an adhesive. For the main part, you have, therefore, already covered the necessary science and its applications as well as the usual materials that are used. Consequently all that needs to be done in this chapter is to pull together those aspects that are important to coatings and to discuss a few topics that are peculiar to coatings – gloss and matt surface finishes for instance.

A useful way of getting to grips with the requirements of coatings is to list the ones that are *in common with those for an adhesive*. As you did in Chapter 1, do this under the headings (a) the requirements of the completed coating, and (b) the requirements of the coating process.

A1 The completed coating
In fact all the requirements of an adhesive are relevant to a coating.

(a) Is it strong enough?
A coating must adhere to the surface of an object, at least so that it is held firmly in place. The adhesive bonding may also need to withstand internal stresses created by any differential thermal expansion between the coating and the underlying material, or by shrinkage. In either case, the coating can break. A coating is often required to be hard – to withstand abrasive wear or to avoid dirt being picked-up – and to be tough. All of these requirements are similar to those already considered for adhesives in Chapter 4.

(b) Can it be removed without damage to the object?
This is a particularly important question for more fragile objects such as paintings, textiles and paper. As with adhesives, the answer is determined by the solubility of the aged coating or its ability to swell and consequently weaken. The numerous problems connected with separation of unwanted material from an object are dealt with in Book 2.

(c) Will it last?
The requirements are similar to those for an adhesive (Chapter 5). The polymeric material is thin and spread over a large area so that it is very exposed to attack by oxidation and light. Since the object must be viewed through the coating it must not discolour nor must it reflect or scatter too much light.

(d) Should it be invisible or obvious?
For coatings used in conservation the answer is usually straightforwardly that it should be transparent, in fact as invisible as possible, in order fully to reveal the object's surface.

(e) Will it harm the object?
The same arguments apply to coatings and adhesives. Objects can be damaged by the release of chemicals from the coating, for example, nitric acid from cellulose nitrate, or by the effects of heat. Molten materials are seldom used as coatings, except perhaps waxes, but coatings that are formed *in situ* by chemical reactions can evolve heat. This heat could be damaging, particularly by accelerating the oxidation processes that discolour pigments, dyes and paper.

A2 The coating process

- For a good result: the surface to be coated should be clean. This, as with adhesives, is necessary for good wetting, and particularly so for coatings, because dirt on the surface will detract from the appearance of the object.

- The applied coating should spread easily. To give the object proper protection, a coating should spread over the whole surface and have a uniform thickness. Again, as with an adhesive, the final product has to be a solid but it is applied more effectively as a liquid with a low surface tension and viscosity, as this avoids brush marks.

B Particular requirements of a coating

As you have seen, many of the basic requirements of a coating are common to those for an adhesive, and, therefore, many of the arguments that have been used in Chapters 3–5 are valid for coatings. However, some coatings need to have certain characteristics not associated with an adhesive. In particular, in conservation work coatings are usually used to protect an object in such a way that its features can be displayed while still providing adequate protection. Consequently its **optical properties** are important; specifically, it should be transparent, and decisions have to be made about whether it should have a gloss or a matt surface finish. In addition, since a coating is usually extremely thin, its effectiveness as a barrier film is of considerable importance. These characteristics will be considered in turn. The very important topic of *refractive index* of coatings will be dealt with in Book 4.

optical properties

(a) Transparency

An object is seen as a result of the light that is reflected by its surface. A transparent coating allows the light passing through it to be reflected by the surface of the object and back through the coating. Colourless polymeric materials can be anything from highly transparent to completely opaque. Any flaw, such as a crack or hole, or inhomogeneity within a coating material **scatters** the light falling on it and therefore decreases its transparency. In a completely opaque coating, no light actually gets through to the surface of the object and thence back to the eye. The difference in the behaviour of light in a transparent and an opaque material is illustrated schematically in Figure 6.1 (overleaf).

light scatter

A flawless, colourless, amorphous polymer is transparent because there are no internal discontinuities to scatter the light passing through it. On the other hand, crystalline polymers are normally opaque or translucent because of the mixture of crystalline and amorphous regions they contain. This tends to mean that if transparency were the only consideration, an homogeneous coating of an amorphous polymer is required.

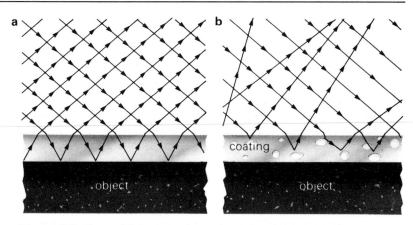

Figure 6.1 *Rays of light **a** passing uninterrupted through a clear coating and **b** being scattered on meeting flaws. (Rays of light reflected from the surface of the coating are not shown.*

(b) Surface finish

gloss surface

Gloss is a term for describing the optical nature of the surface of a material, whether it is transparent or opaque. A very **glossy** surface is one that behaves like a mirror; it is a very flat surface. In contrast a **matt** surface is one that is rough on a small scale, so that light is scattered by the surface irregularities.

matt

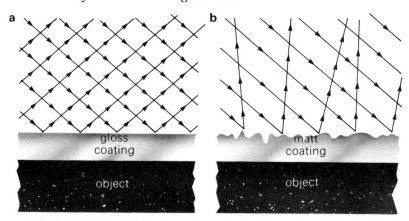

Figure 6.2 *Rays of light being **a** reflected symetrically from a glossy surface and **b** scattered by surface irregularities.*

To obtain the mirror-like surface finish required for a gloss finish, the molecules in the coating must be sufficiently mobile, and have sufficient time, to move so that the surface becomes smooth. This means that the coating must remain above its T_g for long enough to allow polymer movement as the solvent evaporates slowly. The reverse requirements produce a matt finish, that is a quickly evaporating solvent that allows the T_g of the coating to be increased very quickly to above room temperature so that movement is restricted.

matting agent

It is possible to include **matting agents** in a coating. Silica aerogel is an example and its effect is to break up the surface finish by means of the extremely fine particles, exactly as shown in Figure 6.2(b).

(c) Barrier properties

A protective coating can act as a barrier in two ways; to keep an object clean, or to protect it from attack by chemicals in the environment. The former function requires a hard coating that, when necessary, can be cleaned readily. It must also protect against "pollutants" such as water, hydrogen sulphide (H_2S), sulphur dioxide (SO_2) and oxygen that cause tarnishing, oxidation and other forms of corrosion. In order to attack the underlying material, these agents must diffuse through the coating. Ideally, a coating should not be permeable but, as you know from Chapter 5, this is impossible for small molecules in polymeric materials. The problem is made worse by the fact that coatings are usually very thin – typically a small fraction of a millimetre. So to provide the best barrier to diffusion, the molecules in a coating should be packed as close together as possible. In this case, therefore, a crystalline polymer is preferable to an amorphous polymer, and it should be below its glass transition temperature.

As with adhesives, coating materials have to start out in liquid form and end up as a solid. Again, the various types can be classified as melt-freeze, those that depend on drying by evaporation, and those that are cured by chemical reaction(s). The first type is rarely used and is limited to low melting point waxes. The waxes are soft when applied and to get a gloss finish the molecules must be moved and arranged mechanically to produce a mirror-like surface by polishing, which is discussed in Chapter 2 of Book 2.

To illustrate some other important requirements of a coating, and also to continue the application of the polymer chemistry you learnt in Chapter 2, consider a few examples of each of the other two classes of coating materials.

C Solvent coatings

Shellac dissolved in alcohol is one of the oldest coating materials. It is a resin produced by an insect, the lac insect, to protect its eggs. Shellac is a complex mixture of thermoplastic polymers which with ageing develops cross-links and becomes progressively less soluble; thus it becomes increasingly difficult to remove.

shellac

Cellulose nitrate was the first important synthetic lacquer and is still in use. Its structure, and advantages and disadvantages as an adhesive are described in Chapter 3, Section B. As a coating material the solvent normally used is butyl acetate. It shrinks through loss of solvent and plasticiser and thus becomes hard and brittle. It also degrades chemically by releasing small amounts of nitric acid. It is still used, primarily because it is easy to remove. Better chemical and mechanical stability is provided by **acrylic lacquers** which are based on the methacrylate family of polymers such as poly-methyl methacrylate (PMMA); examples are Paraloid B72 and B67 used as picture varnishes. B72 is a co-polymer of methyl acrylate

acrylic lacquers

and ethyl methacrylate. They remain soluble and are easily replaced, and are not affected unduly by light. However, acrylic lacquers that use PMMA are rather stiff and brittle and therefore prone to cracking under internal stresses. This problem can be ameliorated by incorporating a plasticiser but, of course, this will be lost slowly by evaporation.

A better approach is to use other methacrylates in which the methyl ($-CH_3$) side-group on the oxygen atom is replaced by a large hydrocarbon side-group; for instance, a butyl group ($-C_4H_9$) or even a lauryl group ($-C_{12}H_{25}$).

$$\left[-CH_2-\overset{\displaystyle CH_3}{\underset{\displaystyle COOR}{\overset{|}{\underset{|}{C}}}}- \right]_n$$

In this structural formula, R refers to the large side-group, and the *n* outside the brackets means that this unit is repeated a large number of times.

These large side-chains give a high degree of mobility to the molecule because they are themselves flexible, and so they keep the backbone chains of neighbouring molecules further apart. They also make the polymer more soluble in hydrocarbon solvents, since they have a very similar structure and composition to these side-chains (remember "like dissolves like"). As polymers can be made with various proportions of these units fixed onto the main chain, there are enormous variations possible in their composition and properties. These polymer solutions have potentially very satisfactory properties and are widely used in coating metals, oil paintings and other surfaces. For some tasks it is useful to be able to choose an acrylic lacquer using solvents that are not so powerful as to attack the coated material. The long side-chains in poly (lauryl methacrylate) allow it to dissolve in white spirit, which is a relatively innocuous solvent. With shorter side-chains as in poly (butyl methacrylate), rather more powerful and toxic solvents (such as xylene) are required and these may on occasion swell the underlying material or cause dyestuffs to bleed.

A point to be careful about when using a solvent coating on some objects is that it may not fully and properly coat the surface it is meant to protect. After any liquid film has been spread over a rough solid surface, it will not remain of uniform thickness. This is due to surface tension, which as you know, pulls a liquid surface into a curve. This means that the film becomes thinner on the peaks and edges of a surface, (see Figure 6.3). Thus, the areas on the surface most susceptible to damage and chemical attack are barely protected

emulsions   by a coating based on a liquid system. **Emulsions** are more successful in this respect than ordinary solvent coatings. The poly(vinyl acetate) (PVAC) co-polymers that were described in Chapter 3, Section B are

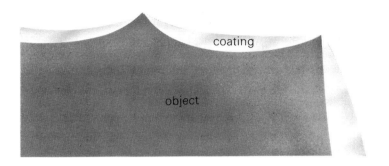

Figure 6.3 *Examples of irregularities in the thickness of a coating caused by edges and protrusions on the surface of an object.*

one of a number of coatings used in the form of an emulsion. Emulsions have the added advantage that the carrier is usually water, which means that they avoid the toxicity and flammability hazards of volatile organic liquids. Another way of tackling the problem is to use liquids with a higher viscosity that react chemically to provide the solid coating.

D Reaction coatings

Like reaction adhesives, reaction coatings involve polymerisation *in situ*. There are two basic types, those in which network polymerisation occurs as they dry out, by means of oxygen in the atmosphere; and those in which the polymerisation occurs by chemical reactions between polymers in the coating material.

The traditional **oil-based** paints are the most important example of the first type. These use natural fatty oils such as linseed, soya and tung, each of which contains a mixture of different long-chain molecules. (They are actually esters formed between glycerol:

oil-based paints

$$CH_2OH$$
$$|$$
$$CHOH$$
$$|$$
$$CH_2OH$$

and various fatty acids. Esters were introduced in Book 1.) These molecules, if straightened out, would be roughly Y-shaped, each arm of the Y containing eighteen or more carbon atoms with one, two or three, carbon–carbon double bonds in the chain. As these oils dry out, oxygen diffuses in and reacts with the double bonds to form cross-links, as illustrated in Figure 6.4. An oxygen atom links two molecues together by utilising one of the bonds in the double bonds. It is very similar to the way sulphur atoms cross-link rubber molecules in the vulcanisation of rubber. In this way the oil is converted into a network polymer which, as more links are formed, becomes progressively more rigid. However, the process is slow, which means that the paint can remain tacky for days, making it liable to pick up dust. With time, the extensive cross-linking which occurs leads to hardness and brittleness. In addition, oxidation reactions with impurities produce molecules with a strong yellow colour. Both of these changes make films of oils like linseed and tung unsatisfactory.

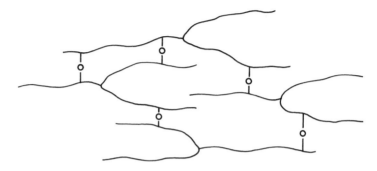

Figure 6.4

A further disadvantage of paints that depend on oxygen for network polymerisation is that the reaction will be more rapid at the surface than in the bulk of the coating – another problem related to diffusion. This can produce surface shrinkage and shrivelling.

Chemical adjustments can be made to the ingredients in these paint formulations to achieve quicker drying and to reduce the amount of oil used, and hence to reduce some of the yellowing. Many **alkyds** such formulations incorporate polymers called **alkyds** which are a form of polyester (see Chapter 2, Section A).

The other type of reaction coating, those involving network polymerisation between components in the coating mixture, are similar to reaction adhesives. The kinds most commonly used are based on epoxy resins, polyurethane, and urea formaldehyde. Having studied this book, you should be equipped to make sense of other texts that deal with them.

7

Consolidants

Consolidants

Consolidation is widely used in conservation as a means of imparting structural strength to an object that has deteriorated and is in danger of disintegrating; crumbling stonework, decaying canvasses used in painting and worm-eaten wood are examples. In a material requiring consolidation, many of the primary and/or secondary bonds that hold it together have been broken, to the point where the structure can no longer support its own weight (or any other forces it has to resist) and retain its shape. For these reasons worm-eaten wood becomes soft and spongy to the touch, and deteriorated stone crumbles away to a powder. Consolidation is an artificial way of repairing the damage caused by what are, after all, natural processes.

The first requirements of a consolidating material (a **consolidant**) are that it can impregnate the object and impart strength by binding it together – in other words, it must act like an adhesive. In fact, thinking about consolidants is very much like thinking about adhesives in three dimensions. To avoid going through all the questions previously asked of adhesives and coatings, you could simply ask which of the requirements for an adhesive joint, and the jointing process, are *not* requirements for a consolidant or the process of applying a consolidant.

By using Figure 1.3 in Chapter 1 (or the answers to the equivalent task in Chapter 6) as a check-list, you should have found that the answer is simple: that all the requirements for an adhesive and for the jointing process are relevant to consolidation. However, a bit more attention needs to be given to the consolidation process because the requirements are rather more stringent than for adhesives. In joining or coating care has to be taken to ensure that the

consolidant

adhesive covers the whole of the surface involved. This, of course, applies in consolidation, but achieving it is rather more difficult.

Clearly, for reasons identical to those for adhesives and coatings, a consolidant has to start out in liquid form and end up as a solid. However, the liquid may have to penetrate very long, tiny crevices and pores in an object, and this makes the task of a consolidant more demanding.

It is necessary for a consolidant to wet the surface of the material on which it is being used, not only to make a satisfactory adhesive bond, but also to enable it to penetrate the object. If you visualise a porous solid as a bundle of capillary tubes, you can appreciate that a liquid consolidant will be drawn into a porous material by means of capillary action.

Although the surface tension determines the extent to which a consolidating liquid penetrates a porous solid, other factors affect the rate of penetration. The two main ones are the viscosity of the liquid and the size of the pores. Let us consider these in turn.

A Viscosity

viscosity

As you know from Chapter 1, Section B (and Book 2), the viscosity of a liquid is a measure of its mobility (runniness); water is more mobile (less viscous) than treacle. When a liquid flows, its molecules slide over one another. This is a process of shear, and **viscosity** is, essentially, a measure of the rate at which shear strain occurs under a shear stress. In the absence of other sources, such as an applied pressure, the shear stress is provided by the force of gravity – which is why rivers run down to the sea, water flows over a waterfall, and why you can pour milk from a jug. Clearly the stronger the bonds between the atoms or molecules in a liquid, the smaller will be the shear strain produced by a given shear stress; in other words the more viscous it will be.

Figure 7.1 lists the viscosities of a wide range of liquids at room temperature. The units have been chosen for easy comparison with the best-known liquid, water, which has a value of 1.0*. Notice the enormously wide range between, say, bitumen and ether. It is also interesting to note that ether is less viscous than water; this is because the secondary (hydrogen) bonding in water is stronger than in ether (see Book 2).

The viscosity of all liquids decreases as the temperature is raised; they become more runny. This is why, for example, car oil flows more freely when the engine is warm. This effect is another illustration of the effect of heat on a process. With increasing temperature a material gains more thermal energy. This means that there is an increasing probability that thermal activation will overcome the

---

*·*Traditionally, viscosity was measured in* **poise** *(after the nineteenth-century doctor and scientist Poiseuille). In the SI system, the units are newton seconds per square metre* (Nsm^{-2})*.*

Material	Viscosity at 20°C $(\mathrm{Nsm}^{-2} \times 10^{-3})$
amorphous polymer (T_g, 20°C)	10^{15}
amorphous polymer (T_g, 0°C)	10^{10}
"solid" pitch or bitumen	10^{11}
treacle	5000
glycerine	1500
castor oil	1000
linseed oil	30
epoxy resin (uncured)	15–25
ethyl alcohol	1.2
water	1.0
triethoxymethylsilane	0.6
trimethoxymethylsilane	0.5
diethyl ether	0.2

Figure 7.1

bonding between molecules. You could carry out for yourself a demonstration showing the influence of viscosity on the rate at which a liquid penetrates a crack or pore.

Demonstration

Fill two beakers with a fairly viscous liquid such as glycerine, and heat one of them to about 100°C. Place an identical capillary tube in each beaker and observe what happens. The hot glycerine will rise up the tube very quickly; the cool glycerine rises very slowly but will eventually reach the same height.

The *height* to which a liquid rises in a capillary is determined by the surface tension (the surface tension of a liquid decreases with increasing temperature, so the capillary rise for hot glycerine will be a bit less than that of the cool glycerine). The *rate* at which the liquid rises to that height is determined by the viscosity.

Therefore, to achieve good penetration of an object by a con-solidant, a liquid of *high surface tension* and *low viscosity* is desirable. The practical benefits of raising the temperature of the liquid to achieve lower viscosity in conservation treatments are dubious because it is often difficult to heat an object without damaging it.

As a first step consider viscosity in terms of symbols. Quantitatively, you can say that the amount of liquid passing into a porous medium in one second (call it Q), is *inversely proportional* to its viscosity, which may be called η (the Greek letter *eta*). That is:

$$Q \propto \frac{1}{\eta}$$

Here $\propto$ is a proportionality sign; it means Q is proportional to $1/\eta$ or, "there is a direct relationship between Q and $1/\eta$." As η gets bigger, $1/\eta$ gets smaller and so Q gets proportionally smaller (this is called "inversely proportional"). The formula simply describes what you would expect, that is that the rate of flow (Q) increases as viscosity (η) decreases; water flows more rapidly than oil, for instance. You can check this mathematically for yourself by putting some values of η from Figure 7.1 into the formula; the larger the value of η, the lower the value of Q.

The extent and rate at which a liquid penetrates a porous material depends on the characteristics of the material as well as those of the liquid, in particular on its *porosity*.

B Porosity

The porosity of a substance may be thought of as the percentage of pore space in the total volume – that is, the space not occupied by solid matter. It is possible that not all the pores are connected with one another or with the surface, so they may not be accessible to the **effective porosity** liquid consolidant. The **effective porosity** is the pore space connecting directly or indirectly with the surface and clearly, for good consolidation the effective porosity should be as high as possible. With wood, for example, decayed organic matter often blocks the pores or narrows their width thus making effective consolidation less easy. Figure 7.2 shows a block of stone with about 50 per cent porosity but only about 20 per cent effective porosity.

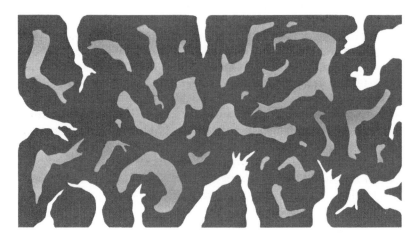

Figure 7.2 *Cross-section through porous stone. Pores with both ends closed are shown shaded.*

Typical values for the porosity of sandstones are 15–30 per cent and for limestones 5–15 per cent. The extent and rate of penetration of a porous medium by a liquid also depends on whether the liquid is forced in under *pressure* or not, and on the dimensions of the pores.

The rate of flow can be increased by exerting a pressure on it. Pressure is similar to stress in that it is a force acting over an area, and it has the same units, Nm^{-2} in SI. The effect of pressure is obvious; you can remove the liquid in a tube, such as a straw, much more quickly by blowing down the tube. You also have to suck harder on a straw dipped in a viscous milk shake than in a glass of lemonade. In each case you are effectively overcoming the viscosity of the liquid by exerting pressure.

For similar reasons, to raise a specified volume of liquid through a straw you would have to suck harder on a long straw or a thin one than on a short one or a wide one. So the *rate of flow* of a liquid also depends on the cross-sectional area and the length of a pore.

C Factors affecting penetration of the consolidant

Having established that the rate of flow of a liquid in a porous material increases with pressure and also that it increases with the cross-sectional area of a pore, you know that as the *viscosity* of the liquid increases or as the *length* of the pore increases, the rate of flow *decreases*. The degree to which the flow rate actually varies through changes in pore dimension, pressure and viscosity of liquid is an intrinsic property of the porous medium and is called its **per-**   **permeability**
meability. If the permeability of a solid is zero then there can be no flow and the substance is said to be **impermeable** or impervious. Some of the factors that affect permeability were discussed in Chapter 5 when looking at the transport of vapour through a polymer.

Since the intrinsic permeability of the object you may want to consolidate cannot be changed, other factors will have to be varied. The dimensions of pores in the object are predetermined and so only viscosity and pressure remain as variables. Viscosity can be altered by choice of material, by dilution in a less viscous solvent and by temperature change. Seeking ways of changing the pressure has led to the adoption of various consolidation processes such as **vacuum**   **vacuum impregnation**
impregnation in its different forms; details of the techniques that have been used can be found in the conservation literature. Do not forget that the force of gravity can also be used to promote consolidation, since a liquid is able to percolate down into a porous body due to the gravitational pull exerted on it by the Earth.

D Consolidation methods

A consolidant has to be applied as a liquid and, as you know by now, there are three ways of doing this: melt-freeze, evaporation of a solvent carrier, and chemical reaction between consolidant liquids.

The first method has very limited application for deep penetration because most materials that could be used, waxes for example, have high viscosities when molten, and, further, their viscosity increases as they cool – which they will do rapidly as they penetrate an object. The high temperatures necessary to keep wax molten during impregnation may damage the object.

Consolidation using solids in solution is a common technique, and in most cases the solid is a polymeric material dissolved in water or an organic solvent. This is, of course, a convenient way of reducing the viscosity; the main drawback is that the consolidant tends to be drawn back to the surface of the object as the solvent evaporates. This effect is the result of capillary action. Figure 7.3(a) shows a pore which has been penetrated by a consolidant in solution. On ceasing the impregnation process, the solvent begins to evaporate from the pore entrance. Due to the capillary action, the column of solution rises up the pore, just as it would rise up a capillary tube (see Chapter 1, Section B).

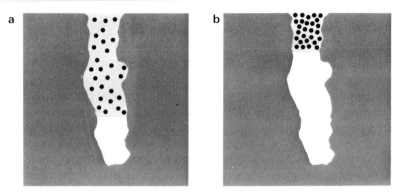

Figure 7.3 a *Solvent in pore immediately after treatment.*
b *Consolidant concentrated at mouth of pore after evaporation.*

Problems can also arise because the evaporation of solvent can cause the collapse of fragile materials, such as the cell walls in organic materials. Waterlogged wood is a case in point. The cell walls are so weak that when the water is removed they shrink and collapse under the resulting internal stresses unless they are supported by solid consolidant. During consolidation, the surface tension of the solvent can also rupture the cell walls. You can illustrate this happening for yourself.

Demonstration
Tie a piece of thread loosely across the diameter of a small loop of metal wire, such as that used by children for blowing bubbles. Dip the loop into a soap solution to form a soap film on it. The thread will lie loosely in the soap film, Figure 7.4(a). Now burst the film on one side of the thread and observe what happens to the thread. It is pulled taut, see Figure 7.4(b), by the surface tension acting on the thread. Molecules some distance away from the thread will experience a pull in all directions lying in the film due to the bonding forces with other molecules. However, those near the thread experience a net pull away from the thread because the molecules on the far side of the thread are missing – there will be no counterbalancing pull, Figure 7.4(c).

surface tension damage   The same effect occurs when the solvent evaporates from the pores in a piece of wood. The **surface tension** can be high enough to exceed the strength of the cell walls and therefore break them. For this reason the solvent used should have as low a surface tension as

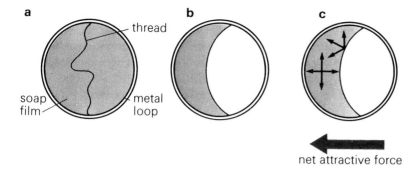

thread

soap film

metal loop

net attractive force

Figure 7.4

possible. For example rosin dissolved in acetone which has a low surface tension has been used to consolidate waterlogged wood.

Another common consolidant is **polyethylene glycol** (PEG), a long-chain polymer with a structural formula of the type:

$$HO-\underset{\underset{H}{|}}{\overset{\overset{H}{|}}{C}}\overbrace{-\underset{\underset{H}{|}}{\overset{\overset{H}{|}}{C}}-O-\underset{\underset{H}{|}}{\overset{\overset{H}{|}}{C}}}^{\text{repeat unit}}-\cdots-\underset{\underset{H}{|}}{\overset{\overset{H}{|}}{C}}-O-\underset{\underset{H}{|}}{\overset{\overset{H}{|}}{C}}-\underset{\underset{H}{|}}{\overset{\overset{H}{|}}{C}}-OH$$

polyethylene glycol

Polyethylene glycol (PEG) is a good consolidant for wood because it will readily form hydrogen-bonds to cellulose. With stone, however, it is less successful since there is no possibility of the formation of hydrogen-bonds. There are many varieties identified by their molecular mass, for example, PEG 1500 which has a molecular mass of 1500 has approximately 34 repeats. Although used in water it does not cause surface tension damage because consolidation has effectively taken place before evaporation occurs.

As with reaction adhesives and coatings, consolidation can also be achieved by liquids that react to form a solid product *in situ*. Epoxy resins are an example. In the form in which they are generally available the two components may be too viscous to achieve significant penetration and they have to be dissolved in a suitable solvent. This can lead to a problem because some of the components of the consolidation mixture can be attracted more strongly to the material of the object than others; this will depend on the relative strength of the secondary bonding forces of the different consolidant molecules and those of the object. If the difference is significant, the components become separated and are not then all available in the required location to react to form the solid polymer.

This disadvantage is overcome if the components do not need dilution by solvent. One means of achieving this is by adjusting the chemical structure of the molecules involved so that a low viscosity is possible; epoxy resins are now commercially available with satisfactorily low viscosities.

organosilanes   One way of ensuring a low viscosity is to have the consolidant initially in a form with the lowest possible molecular mass, that is, as the monomer from which the polymer network is created. A good example of this is the **organosilane** range of stone consolidants. These simple organic compounds of silicon have a very low viscosity (see Figure 7.1) so that deep penetration is easily achieved. They have the ability to react with water to produce extensive network polymers. Figure 7.5 gives an idea of how the network is built up from molecules of trimethoxymethylsilane.

$$\underset{\underset{\displaystyle OCH_3}{|}}{\overset{\overset{\displaystyle OCH_3}{|}}{CH_3{-}Si{-}OCH_3}} + H_2O \longrightarrow \underset{\underset{\displaystyle OCH_3}{|}}{\overset{\overset{\displaystyle OCH_3}{|}}{CH_3{-}Si{-}OH}} + CH_3OH$$

trimethoxymethylsilane

$$\underset{\underset{\displaystyle OCH_3}{|}}{\overset{\overset{\displaystyle OCH_3}{|}}{CH_3{-}Si{-}OH}} + \underset{\underset{\displaystyle OCH_3}{|}}{\overset{\overset{\displaystyle OCH_3}{|}}{HO{-}Si{-}CH_3}} \longrightarrow \underset{\underset{\displaystyle OCH_3\ \ OCH_3}{|\quad|}}{\overset{\overset{\displaystyle OCH_3\ \ OCH_3}{|\quad|}}{CH_3{-}Si{-}O{-}Si{-}CH_3}} + H_2O$$

$$\underset{\underset{\displaystyle OCH_3\ \ OCH_3}{|\quad|}}{\overset{\overset{\displaystyle OCH_3\ \ OCH_3}{|\quad|}}{CH_3{-}Si{-}O{-}Si{-}CH_3}} + H_2O \longrightarrow \underset{\underset{\displaystyle OCH_3\ \ OCH_3}{|\quad|}}{\overset{\overset{\displaystyle OCH_3\ \ OH}{|\quad|}}{CH_3{-}Si{-}O{-}Si{-}CH_3}} + CH_3OH$$

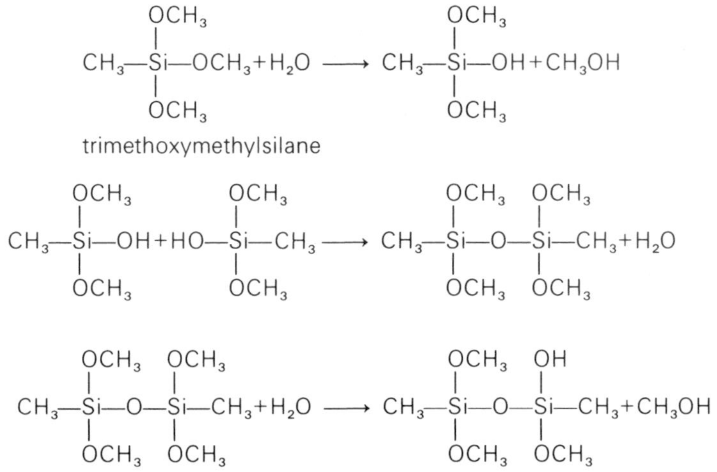

Figure 7.5 *The process by which molecules of trimethoxymethylsilane build up to form a network.*

In the course of the polymerisation, reaction can take place either between a water molecule and a methoxy group ($-OCH_3$) with elimination of a methanol molecule and formation of an hydroxyl group ($-OH$), as illustrated in the final sequence of Figure 7.5, or between two newly formed hydroxyl groups with elimination of a water molecule (the second sequence in Figure 7.5); compare this with the silicone in Figure 2.6. Notice that in this way water is produced and consumed. As a result, $Si-O-C$ linkages are progessively converted into $Si-O-Si$ linkages and a polymer network which has some similarity to the extremely chemically stable compound, silica, is built-up.

The extent of the polymer network will depend on the precise course which the reaction follows. As the reaction proceeds, the liquid monomer is converted to a solid polymer which shrinks back onto the pore walls and binds the stonework together.

The consolidant does not have to be a covalently bonded chain or network such as an acrylic or siloxane polymer. Stone can also be impregnated with a solution of calcium hydroxide in water. This slowly reacts with carbon dioxide from the atmosphere to form calcium carbonate, an ionic consolidant. (The very low viscosity of a gas, carbon dioxide in this instance, ensures that it can penetrate deep into the pores of the stone.)

One danger of consolidation by means of chemical reaction is the tendency of some chemical reactions to liberate heat. If the quantity of heat evolved during consolidation is great, the safety of a friable object could be endangered.

Both this chapter and Chapter 6 have consistently referred you back to the science contained in the preceding chapters. You have needed to use your understanding of scientific principles to inform your study of the closely related applications of joining, coating and consolidation. This book, and Books 1 and 2 of the series, have covered a wide range of basic science relevant to conservation practice and have concentrated, except in a few unavoidable instances, on a non-quantitative (that is, a non-mathematical) approach. However, in order to proceed further into the sometimes very complex processes which underlie the causes of deterioration and the conservator's treatment of them, it will be necessary to become familiar with some basic applied maths. Because for many people maths can be a prime source of alienation and confusion, some useful maths will be dealt with very simply in Book 4. This book will allow you the chance to revise topics already covered and help you to elucidate the conservation literature which deals with measurement and the interpretation of experimental data.

Acknowledgements

This series has been prepared by a team of conservation scientists, conservators and science teachers. The Crafts Council is indebted to the conservators and, in particular, the conservation scientists who have given so much of their time to this book's preparation over the last three years. The Council also wishes to acknowledge the generosity of the institutions and private workshops (especially the British Museum, the Open University, Glasgow Art Gallery and Museum, and the Museum of London) who have given their support by allowing their staff to work with us. In particular, the Council owes special thanks to Jonathan Ashley-Smith for his contribution as scientific editor.

February 1984

Answers

Chapter 4

1   The stress is greatest at the smallest cross-section, this is at B.

2 **a** Strain is given by $\dfrac{\text{change in length}}{\text{original length}}$. In this case, all of the rods had the same original length and since that in (a) has clearly stretched the most, it has undergone the greatest strain.

2 **b** Young's modulus is given by stress divided by strain. Since (c) has twice the cross-sectional area of (a), the stress produced in (c) is half that of (a). If the change in length of (c) were half that of (a), the strain in (c) would be half that of (a), and the values of Young's modulus would be the same for both materials. But since the strain in (c) is clearly less than half that of (a) (it is more resistant to deformation), it has the higher Young's modulus.

Photographic credits

Recommended reading

Conservation science is a comparatively young discipline which has yet to develop a distinctive literature of its own. There are relatively few dedicated textbooks, and most advances in knowledge and techniques are to be found in conference preprints and proceedings and in journal articles. One consequence is that conservation students, perhaps more than others, have to ferret out the literature they require. Another is that it is not possible to present here a bibliography which precisely matches the material in this book, topic by topic.

Listed below is a selection of English language works from conservation and other disciplines which are likely to be most rewarding. They should be available in any well-equipped conservation library. The individual papers contained within them, in the journals listed and indeed in the wider international conservation literature, can be located with the help of Art and Archaeology Technical Abstracts and/or on-line via the Conservation Information Network. The latter also offers a materials database which provides technical data on conservation materials, using many of the concepts explained in this book.

International Institute for Conservation (IIC) Publications

Congress preprints:

Preprints for the IIC Rome Conference 1961 (bound volume of conference papers distributed to delegates); published as *Recent Advances in Conservation*, edited by G. Thomson, Butterworth, London, 1963.

Preprints for the IIC Delft Conference 1964 (bound volume of conference papers distributed to delegates); a fuller version in similar format appeared as *IIC 1964 Delft Conference on the Conservation of Textiles Collected Preprints*, 2nd edition, IIC, London, 1965; published as *Textile Conservation*, edited by Jentina E. Leene, Butterworth, London, 1972.

Preprints for the contributions to the London Conference on *Museum Climatology*, edited by Garry Thomson, IIC, London, 1967; revised edition May 1968.

Preprints for the contributions to the New York Conference on *Conservation of Stone and Wooden Objects*, IIC, London, 1970; second edition, edited by Garry Thomson, published in two volumes, Volume 1 *Stone*, Volume 2 *Wooden Objects*, August 1972; subsequently reprinted as a single volume.

Conservation of Paintings and the Graphic Arts, preprints for the contributions to the Lisbon Congress 1972, IIC, London, 1972; published as *Conservation and Restoration of Pictorial Art*, edited by Norman Brommelle and Perry Smith, Butterworth, London, 1976.

Conservation in Archaeology and the Applied Arts, preprints for the contributions to the Stockholm Congress 1975, IIC, London, 1975.

Conservation of Wood in Painting and the Decorative Arts, preprints for the contributions to the Oxford Congress, edited by N. S. Brommelle, Anne Moncrieff and Perry Smith, IIC, London, 1978.

Conservation Within Historic Buildings, preprints for the contributions to the Vienna Congress, edited by N. S. Brommelle, Garry Thomson and Perry Smith, IIC, London, 1980.

Science and Technology in the Service of Conservation, preprints for the contributions to the Washington Congress, edited by N. S. Brommelle and Garry Thomson, IIC, London, 1982.

Adhesives and Consolidants, preprints for the contributions to the Paris Congress, edited by N. S. Brommelle, Elizabeth M. Pye, Perry Smith and Garry Thomson, IIC, London, 1984.

Adhésifs et Consolidants, Edition française des communications, IIC Xe Congrès International, publiée par la Section Française de l'IIC, Champs-sur-Marne, 1984.

Case Studies in the Conservation of Stone and Wall Paintings, preprints for the contributions to the Bologna Congress, edited by N. S. Brommelle and Perry Smith, IIC, London, 1986.

The Conservation of Far Eastern Art, preprints for the contributions to the Kyoto Congress, edited by John S. Mills, Perry Smith and Kazuo Yamasaki, IIC, London, 1988.

Conservation of Far Eastern Art, abstracts of the contributions to the Kyoto Congress, edited by H. Mabuchi and Perry Smith, Japanese Organizing Committee of the IIC Kyoto Congress, Tokyo, 1968.

Cleaning, Retouching and Coatings: Technology and Practice for Easel Paintings and Polychrome Sculpture, preprints for the contributions to the Brussels Congress, edited by John S. Mills and Perry Smith, IIC, London, 1990.

Cleaning, Retouching and Coatings, summaries of the posters at the Brussels Congress, IIC, London, 1990.

Conservation of the Iberian and Latin American Cultural Heritage, preprints for the contributions to the Madrid Congress, edited by H. W. M. Hodges, John S. Mills and Perry Smith, IIC, London, 1992. An abstracts booklet and a Spanish translation of the preprint volume are also planned.

Preventive Conservation: Practice Theory and Research, edited by Ray Ashok and Perry Smith, IIC, London, 1994.

ICOM Committee for Conservation

Proceedings of the following triennial meetings: (1966, 1969 and 1972 were not issued as preprints or subsequently published)

4th Triennial Meeting, Venice – 1975.
5th Triennial Meeting, Zagreb – 1978.
6th Triennial Meeting, Ottawa – 1981.
7th Triennial Meeting, Copenhagen – 1984, Diana de Froment (ed.), Paris: ICOM and the J. Paul Getty Trust.
8th Triennial Meeting, Sydney – 1987, Kirsten Grimstad (ed.), Los Angeles: ICOM CC and the Getty Conservation Institute.
9th Triennial Meeting, Dresden – 1990, J. Cliff McCawley (ed.), Los Angeles: ICOM and the Getty Conservation Institute.

United Kingdom Institute for Conservation (UKIC) Publications

Occasional Papers Series:

No. 1 *Conservation, Archaeology and Museums* (1980).

No. 2 *Microscopy in Archaeological Conservation* (1980).

No. 3 *Lead and Tin: Studies in Conservation and Technology* (1982).

No. 4 *Corrosion Inhibitors in Conservation* (1985).

No. 5 *Archaeological Bone, Antler and Ivory* (1987).

No. 6 *Restoration of Early Musical Instruments* (1987).

No. 7 *From Pinheads to Hanging Bowls: The Identification, Deterioration and Conservation of Applied Enamel and Glass Decoration on Archaeological Artifacts* (1987).

No. 8 *Evidence Preserved in Corrosion Products* (1989).

No. 9 *Conservation of Stained Glass* (1989).

No. 10 *Archaeological Textiles* (1990).

Booth, P., L. Carlyle, M. Davies, C. Leback-Sitwell, N. Kalinsky, A. Southall, V. Todd and J. Townsend, *Appearance, Opinion, Change: Evaluating the Look of Paintings*, reprint of papers given at the conference held jointly by UKIC and The Tate Gallery in January 1990, London: UKIC.

Budden, S. (ed.), *Gilding and Surface Decoration*, London: UKIC.

Entwistle, R., V. Kemp, J. Marsden and V. Todd (eds) (1992) *Life After Death: The Practical Conservation of Natural History Collections*, UKIC/Ipswich Borough Council Conference, February 1992, London: UKIC.

Fairbrass, S. and J. Hermans (eds) (1989) *Modern Art: The Restoration and Techniques of Modern Paper and Paints*, London: UKIC.

Hackney, S., J. Townsend and N. Easthaugh (eds) (1990) *Dirt and Pictures Separated*, London: UKIC.

Norman, M. and V. Todd (eds) (1991) *Storage*, preprints for the UKIC Conference, October 1991, London: UKIC.

Todd, V. (ed.) (1988) *Conservation Today*, preprints for the 30th Anniversary Conference of UKIC held in October 1988, London: UKIC.

ICCROM Publications

Masschelein-Kleiner, L. (1985) *Ancient Binding Media, Varnishes and Adhesives*, Rome: ICCROM.

Torraca, G. (1963) *Synthetic Materials used in the Conservation of Cultural Property* (4th edn 1990), Rome: ICCROM.

Torraca, G. (1975) *Solubility and Solvents for Conservation Problems* (3rd edn 1984), Rome: ICCROM.

Torraca, G. (1981) *Porous Building Materials: Materials Science for Architectural Conservation* (3rd rev. edn 1988), Rome: ICCROM.

Safety literature

Bretherick, L. (ed.) (1986) *Hazards in the Chemical Laboratory*, 4th edn, London: Royal Society of Chemistry.

Clydesdale, A. (1982) *Chemicals in Conservation: A Guide to Possible Hazards and Safe Use* (2nd edn 1987), Edinburgh: Conservation Bureau (Scottish Development Agency) and Scottish Society for Conservation and Restoration.

Howie, F. (ed.) (1987) *Safety in Museums and Galleries*, London: Butterworth with the International Journal of Museum Management.

The Health and Safety Commission (HSC) and the Health and Safety Executive publish a great deal of information which is of interest to conservators. This includes: HSE Guidance Notes Series, Health and Safety (Guidance) Series and Health and Safety (Regulations) Series.

Many are available free of charge from the HSE. Contact HSE Publications Point, St Hugh's House, Stanley Precinct, Bootle, Merseyside L20 3LZ

A full list of current HSC/E publications "Publications in Series" is published twice yearly and is available from HSE Public Enquiry Points:

Baynards House	Broad Lane	(This list applies to the
1 Chepstow Place	Sheffield S3 7HQ	UK; most other countries
Westbourne Grove		have their own safety
London W2 4TF		organisation.)

Other publications

Allsop, Dennis and K. J. Seal (1986) *Introduction to Biodeterioration*, London: Edward Arnold.

Black, J. (ed.) (1987) *Recent Advances in the Conservation and Analysis of Artifacts*, Proceedings of the Jubilee Conservation Conference of the University of London Institute of Archaeology, London: Summer Schools Press.

Brill, T. (1980) *Light: Its Interaction with Art and Antiques*, New York: Plenum Press.

Brown, B. F., H. C. Burnett, W. T. Chase, M. Goodway, J. Kruger and M. Pourbaix (eds) (1977) *Corrosion and Metal Artifacts – a Dialogue between Conservators, Archaeologists and Corrosion Scientists*, National Bureau of Standards Special Publication 479, Washington: US Department of Commerce.

Brydson, J. A. (1989) *Plastics Materials* (5th edn), London: Butterworth.

Burns, R. M. and W. W. Bradley (1962) *Protective Coatings for Metals* (3rd edn 1967), New York: Reinhold.

Cassar, M. (1995) *Environmental Management: Guidelines for Museums and Galleries*, London: Museums & Galleries Commission and Routledge.

Cotterill, R. (1985) *The Cambridge Guide to the Material World*, Cambridge: Cambridge University Press.

Dana, E. S. (1991) *A Textbook of Mineralogy* (5th edn), New York: Wiley.

Eaton, L. and C. Meredith (eds) (1988) *Modern Organic Materials*, preprints for meeting held in Edinburgh, April 1988, Edinburgh: Scottish Society for Conservation and Restoration.

Feller, R. L. (1986) *Artists' Pigments: a Handbook of their History and Characteristics* vol. 1, Washington: National Gallery of Art, Cambridge: Cambridge University Press.

Feller, R. L., N. Stolow and E. H. Jones (1985) *On Picture Varnishes and their Solvents*, Washington: National Gallery of Art.

Fleming, D., C. Paine and J. Rhodes (eds) (1992) *Social History in Museums: a Manual of Curatorship*, London: HMSO.

Franks, F. (1983) *Water* (rev. edn 1984), London: Royal Society of Chemistry.

Gettens, R. J. and G. L. Stout (1966) *Painting Materials: a Short Encyclopedia*, 2nd edn, New York: Dover Publications.

Gordon, J. E. (1968) *The New Science of Strong Materials*, Harmondsworth: Penguin.

Green, L. R. and D. Thickett (1995) 'Testing materials for use in the storage and display of antiquities. Revised methodology', *Studies in Conservation* 40.

Harley, R. D. (1980) *Artists' Pigments c. 1600–1835: a Study in Documentary Sources* (2nd edn 1982), London: Butterworth.

Hodges, H. (1964) *Artifacts – an Introduction to Early Materials and Technology* (3rd edn 1989), London: Duckworth.

Horie, C. V. (1987) *Materials for Conservation*, Sevenoaks: Butterworth.

Knell, S. (ed.) (1994) *Care of Collections*, London: Routledge.

Leigh, G. J. (1971) *Nomenclature of Inorganic Chemistry, Definitive Rules 1970* (3rd edn 1971), Oxford: Blackwell.

Long, P. and R. Levering (eds) (1979) *Paper – Art and Technology*, San Francisco: World Print Council.

Mayer, R. M. (1970) *The Artists' Handbook of Materials and Techniques*, ed. E. Smith (4th edn 1982), London: Faber & Faber.

McCrone, W. C. and J. G. Delly (1973) *The Particle Atlas*, vol. 2, Michigan: Ann Arbor Science.

McCrone, W. C., L. B. McCrone and J. G. Delly (1978) *Polarized Light Microscopy*, Michigan: Ann Arbor Science.

Mills, J. S. and R. White (1987) *The Organic Chemistry of Museum Objects*, London: Butterworth.

Pickwoad, N. (ed.) (1986–8) papers of the 10th anniversary conference, 'New Directions in Paper Conservation', *The Paper Conservator* vols 10–12, Oxford 1986, Worcester: Institute of Paper Conservation.

Rossotti, H. (1975) *Introducing Chemistry*, Harmondsworth: Penguin.

Sandwith, H. and S. Stainton (1993) *The National Trust Manual of Housekeeping*, Harmondsworth: Penguin.

Shields, J. (1970) *Adhesives Handbook*, London: Butterworth.

Street, A. and W. Alexander (1994) *Metals in the Service of Man* (9th edn 1989), Harmondsworth: Penguin.

Tate, J. and J. Townsend (eds) (1987) *SSCR Bulletin 9* (volume devoted to water).

Tate, J. O., N. H. Tennent and J. H. Notman (eds) (1983) *Resins in Conservation*, Proceedings of conference held in May 1982, Edinburgh: Scottish Society for Conservation and Restoration.

Thomson, G. (1978) *The Museum Environment* (2nd edn 1987), London: Butterworth in association with International Institute for Conservation.

See also various publications of:
The Open University, Science Foundation Course, Unit S102
Royal Institute of Chemistry.

Journals, newsletters and conference proceedings of the following organisations:

American Institute for Conservation (AIC)
Australian Institute for the Conservation of Cultural Material (AICCM)

Canadian Conservation Institute (CCI)
Institute of Paper Conservation (IPC)
International Institute for Conservation (IIC)
IIC–Canadian Group
Museums Association (MA)
Scottish Society for Conservation and Restoration (SSCR)
Society for the Preservation of Natural History Collections (SPNHC)
United Kingdom Institute for Conservation (UKIC)

Journals

AICCM Bulletin	*Museum Practice* (MA)
Collection Forum (SPNHC)	*The Paper Conservator* (IPC)
The Conservator (UKIC)	*Restaurator*
Journal of the American Institute for Conservation	*SSCR Journal*
Journal of the IIC–Canadian Group	*Studies in Conservation* (IIC)

Art and Archaeology Technical Abstracts (formerly *IIC Abstracts*), published semi-annually by the Getty Conservation Institute in association with the International Institute for Conservation of Historic and Artistic Works. AATA is an international abstracting journal for conservation.

The *List of Acquisitions* and *Subject Index* are published every two years by ICCROM commencing 1977.

The Conservation Information Network

The Conservation Information Network is an international co-operative project initiated by the Documentation Program of the Getty Conservation Institute (based in California). The Network consists of a series of databases: bibliographic, conservation materials, conservation supplies and equipment databases. These are held on a mainframe computer at the offices of the Canadian Heritage Information Network in Ottawa, Canada. The databases can be accessed via the Canadian Heritage Information Network's World Wide Web Site at http://www.chin.gc.ca. The Network was launched in 1987 and there are over 500 individuals and institutions from around the world subscribing to it. The co-operating partners are: AATA, Conservation Analytical Laboratory of the Smithsonian Institution, ICCROM, ICOMOS, ICOM and CCI. Further information about the Network is available from:

Conservation Information Network,
Communications Canada,
365 Laurier Avenue West,
Journal Tower South, 12th Floor,
Ottawa, Ontario, Canada K1A 0C8

Canadian Heritage Information Network,
Department of Canadian Heritage,
Les Terrasses de la Chaudière,
15 Eddy Street, 4th Floor,
Hull, Quebec, Canada K1A OM5

Within the United Kingdom, information is also available from:

The Conservation Unit, Museums & Galleries Commission,
16 Queen Anne's Gate, London SW1H 9AA

Index